The Biology of Clinical Encounters

T0346635

The Biology of Clinical Encounters

Psychoanalysis as a Science of Mind

John E. Gedo

CRC Press
Taylor & Francis Group
Boca Raton London New York

CRC Press is an imprint of the
Taylor & Francis Group, an **informa** business

First published 1991 by The Analytic Press, Inc.

Published 2018 by CRC Press
Taylor & Francis Group
6000 Broken Sound Parkway NW, Suite 300
Boca Raton, FL 33487-2742

Fisrt issued in paperback 2018

© 1991 by Taylor & Francis Group, LLC
CRC Press is an imprint of Taylor & Francis Group, an Informa business

No claim to original U.S. Government works

ISBN-13: 978-1-138-88157-0 (pbk)
ISBN-13: 978-0-88163-126-5 (hbk)

This book contains information obtained from authentic and highly regarded sources. While all reasonable efforts have been made to publish reliable data and information, neither the author[s] nor the publisher can accept any legal responsibility or liability for any errors or omissions that may be made. The publishers wish to make clear that any views or opinions expressed in this book by individual editors, authors or contributors are personal to them and do not necessarily reflect the views/opinions of the publishers. The information or guidance contained in this book is intended for use by medical, scientific or health-care professionals and is provided strictly as a supplement to the medical or other professional's own judgement, their knowledge of the patient's medical history, relevant manufacturer's instructions and the appropriate best practice guidelines. Because of the rapid advances in medical science, any information or advice on dosages, procedures or diagnoses should be independently verified. The reader is strongly urged to consult the relevant national drug formulary and the drug companies' and device or material manufacturers' printed instructions, and their websites, before administering or utilizing any of the drugs, devices or materials mentioned in this book. This book does not indicate whether a particular treatment is appropriate or suitable for a particular individual. Ultimately it is the sole responsibility of the medical professional to make his or her own professional judgements, so as to advise and treat patients appropriately. The authors and publishers have also attempted to trace the copyright holders of all material reproduced in this publication and apologize to copyright holders if permission to publish in this form has not been obtained. If any copyright material has not been acknowledged please write and let us know so we may rectify in any future reprint.

Visit the Taylor & Francis Web site at
http://www.taylorandfrancis.com

and the CRC Press Web site at
http://www.crcpress.com

Library of Congress Cataloging-in-Publication Data

Gedo, John E.
    Toward a biology of mind / John E. Gedo.
        p. cm.
    Includes bibliographical references and index.
    ISBN 0-88163-126-4
    1. Psychoanalysis. 2. Psychobiology.   I. Title.
    RC506.G43 1991
        616.89'17 – dc20   91-11485
                                                  CIP

For new generations –
from Victoria
to 21st-century granddaughters

TABLE OF CONTENTS

— • ———————————————————————— • —

ACKNOWLEDGMENTS

· ———————————————————— ·

I am grateful to many friends and colleagues for asking me to tackle a number of the specific topics dealt with in this book. In the most direct way, those responsible for "commissioning" some of the chapters were Wagner Bridger, Bertram Cohler, Douglas Detrick, Fred Levin, George Klumpner, George Moraitis, and Arnold Wilson; the Editors of *Psychoanalytic Inquiry* and the Program Committee of the American Psychoanalytic Association asked me to undertake some of the others.

I received important feedback as a result of presenting earlier versions of various chapters to responsive audiences: chapter 2 to Dr. Bridger's Department at the Medical College of Pennsylvania; chapter 4 at the New York Hospital/Cornell Department of Psychiatry, Westchester Division; chapter 5 at the Panel on Obsessional Phenomena of the American Psychoanalytic Association; chapter 6 to the Alumni Association of the University of North Carolina Department of Psychiatry; chapter 7 as a Plenary Address to a Regional Meeting of the Chicago Psychoanalytic Society; chapter 8 in part to a Panel on Psychotherapy and in part at a Meet-the-Author session of the American Psychoanalytic Association; and chapter 12 as a Plenary Address to Division 39 of the American Psychological Association.

Several items appeared previously in other contexts, fortuitously all published by the Analytic Press: chapters 4 and 13 in *Psychoanalytic Inquiry*, chapter 6 in *Psychoanalytic Psychology*, chapter 7 in *The Annual of Psychoanalysis*, chapter 11 in Detrick and Detrick's *Self Psychology: Comparisons and Contrasts*, and chapter 1 as the Introduction to Fred Levin's *Mapping the Mind*.

As has become gratifyingly customary, I am deeply indebted to Paul Stepansky, Editor-in-Chief of the Analytic Press, for his encouragement and substantive suggestions, to Eva Sandberg, my invaluable assistant in manuscript preparation, and to Eleanor Starke Kobrin, for thoughtful copy-editing and shepherding this project to completion.

PREFACE

Throughout my writings, I have consistently adhered to the position that it is not possible to systematize the clinical data obtained through the psychoanalytic method without articulating one's basic biological assumptions, as Sigmund Freud did in proposing a speculative metapsychology. Despite this commitment, I have refrained from going into detail about my own, concentrating instead on an effort to elaborate a nonreductionist yet spare clinical theory (see Gedo, 1991). Even the most "theoretical" of my books, *Models of the Mind* (Gedo & Goldberg, 1973) avoided discussing the issues raised by the uncertain status of Freud's metapsychology, although the discerning reader could infer that I was in the process of repudiating that metatheory from the fact that the crucial concept of psychic energy was left out of account in the book.

In the interval since publication of that monograph, I have tried to make clear that psychoanalytic psychology must solve the problem of simultaneously addressing the realm of mental contents—one of conflictual meanings—and that of psychobiology, i.e., of the mental processes subserving adaptation. A dozen years ago, in *Beyond Interpretation* (Gedo, 1979a), I suggested that the conceptual solution to this problem consists of arranging the totality of personal aims in a hierarchy,

starting with the biological needs of infancy and including both subjective wishes and transitional modes of behavior regulation characterized by oscillation between need and wish.

Although using such a hierarchical model of mentation focuses
analytic attention on derivatives of experiences in the earliest phases of
development – data previously given scant notice in psychoanalytic
discourse – clinical data obtained in the psychoanalytic situation do not
lend themselves to detailed elaboration in terms of reconstructing the
archaic past. The analytic clinician is generally confined to observations about patterned repetitions of behavior – patterns crystallized as
legacies of the transactions of a past that is otherwise unrememberable.
Nonetheless, the need to repeat certain patterns of experience acquired
in the preverbal era of childhood turns these early structuralizations
into organizers of subsequent psychic life. From a slightly different
viewpoint, it might be said that phenomena under the sway of repetition compulsion represent the psychobiological component of human
mental life.

Although I remain convinced that the foregoing considerations
solidly anchored my conceptual work within a biological framework,
as I first claimed a decade ago (Gedo, 1981a, p. 225), I did not command
a knowledge of neurophysiology or cognitive psychology sufficiently
detailed or up-to-date to give the biology of mind the explicit attention
it deserves; through the 1980s my efforts focused on matters of
analytic technique, psychopathology, the creativity question, or the
intellectual history of competing clinical theories within psychoanalysis.

In recent years, much relevant information from cognate disciplines has been made available to psychoanalysts by authors such as
Lichtenberg (1983, 1989), Stern (1985), and Levin (1990), among
others. As a result, I have been able to elaborate my conception of
psychobiology and to reconsider the implications of that conception
for a number of vital issues in our field. The present volume, organized
in four sections, will attempt to articulate this point of view.

I begin with a section describing recent progress toward a biology
of mind. Chapter 1 is an effort to correlate the hierarchical model of
mentation with contemporary neurophysiological understanding; because advances in brain research are so rapid, I have subtitled this
chapter "An Introduction." The second chapter of this section recon-
siders the nature/nurture controversy, demonstrating that the dispute

has generally been framed in meaningless terms. In other words, the biology of mind must simultaneously be viewed from both vantage points, and these should not be counterposed as competing frames of reference.

Section II addresses the issue of clinical syndromes from the biological viewpoint of structured mental processes. Chapter 3 reviews the evolution of the hierarchical model of mental functioning, i.e., the manner in which psychobiology has been represented in my past work. The remaining three chapters in this section deal with syndromes for the understanding of which the biological viewpoint is particularly essential: phobias, obsessions, and affective disturbances. This segment of the book supplements my 1988 volume on psychopathology, *The Mind in Disorder*.

The following section examines the implications of the biological approach for clinical psychoanalysis. Chapter 7 considers the limits placed on psychoanalytic observation by the mutual influence of the participants on each other's mental processes. In chapter 8, I reconsider the significance for our understanding of therapeutics of looking beyond mental contents. Chapter 9 deals with the problem of assessing the clinical evidence produced by analyses informed by a psychobiological orientation. The last chapter in this section compares the outcome of analyses I have conducted in accord with this orientation with the outcomes of my earlier clinical work.

Section IV returns to a theme I have several times discussed in the past: the impact of the current *Zeitgeist*, specifically within the American scene, on the development and reception of analytic ideas. In chapter 11, I examine the most influential movement of the recent analytic past, Self Psychology, from the vantage point of the views put forth in this volume. Chapter 12 attempts to assess the effect of the intellectual currents prevalent in America on the fate of psychoanalysis in this country. The final chapter is my effort to emulate Cassandra in outlining the current perils facing the analytic citadel.

I

Toward the Biology of Mind

CHAPTER 1

·———————————————·

The Biology of Mind
An Introduction

Beyond therapeutic concerns, Sigmund Freud strove to develop psychoanalysis as the basic science of mental functions. Schooled by Brücke, Meynert, and Breuer as a physiological researcher, Freud was alert from the first to the necessity of finding a conceptual bridge between his observations of behavioral phenomena and the prevailing knowledge about the activities of the brain. As early as 1891, he postulated such a link in proposing the hypothesis of "psychic energy," a notion very much in the spirit of the scientific avant-garde of the day.

As a biologist, Freud was not merely a Darwinian, as Sulloway (1979) has cogently demonstrated, he was also a faithful adherent of the school of Helmholtz, one of the founders of which was Freud's admired mentor, Brücke. The program of this scientific movement was the establishment of the life sciences on a solid basis of physics and chemistry–to put this in another way, the banishment of the last vestiges of vitalism from the realms of science. We may judge the seriousness of Freud's commitment to this enterprise from the pleas he was to make to C. G. Jung while the latter was in the process of defining his disagreements with psychoanalysis (see Gedo, 1983, chap. 13): Freud claimed that his theoretical proposals were an essential bulwark against the tendency of psychological systems to lapse into "occultism" – his pejorative designation for Platonic notions about the human soul.

We would therefore do well to look upon such Freudian concepts as psychic energy – the entire system of hypotheses he preferred to call "metapsychology" – as provisional proposals, made within a materialist framework. In this connection, it should be remembered that, as late as 1895, Freud made a heroic, albeit unsuccessful, effort to ground psychology scientifically through a description in terms of putative processes in the nervous system. Freud had to abandon this "Project for a Scientific Psychology" because his understanding of neurophysiology, although completely up-to-date, was far from being equal to the task of undergirding psychology. The subsequent development of psychoanalytic theory on the basis of an entirely speculative metapsychology lacking in empirical referents was a desperate expedient – perhaps more indicative of Freud's need to anchor his thinking within the outward forms expected of a scientific enterprise than it was heuristically useful.

It might also be claimed that Freud's metapsychology maintained its plausibility for generations without obstructing progress in the clinical theory of psychoanalysis, although such progress has required major metapsychological revisions from time to time – theoretical revolutions such as Freud's own reformulation of his drive theories in 1920 and of his principal model of the mind in 1923, or, in the era following Freud's death, the evolution of "ego psychology" under the leadership of Heinz Hartmann (1964; see also Hartmann, Kris, and Loewenstein, 1964). As I have tried to demonstrate elsewhere (Gedo, 1986), those analytic clinicians who made the boldest attempts to extend the applicability of psychoanalysis to populations beyond the boundaries of "neurosis" proper – Ferenczi in the direction of syndromes of a more primitive variety, Melanie Klein in that of early childhood as well as of psychosis – were able to do so only by disregarding the requirement of theoretical coherence. In other words, over the years, more and more clinical observations were accumulated that would have been very difficult to reconcile with the prevalent theoretical schema had anyone made the effort to reestablish a unitary theory for psychoanalysis.

It was David Rapaport (1967) who first noted the resultant theoretical incoherence; he pointed out that the theories of object relations (which were proposed to systematize the clinical findings that did not seem to be explicable in terms of earlier schemata) could not be correlated with the drive theories that form the core of Freudian metapsychology.[1] Probably as a result of Rapaport's scientific rigor, it fell to his students to propose that the best way out of this quandary was the abandonment of the metapsychological paradigm (see George Klein, 1976; Schafer, 1976; Gill and Holzman, 1976). Most of these radicals chose to abandon the biological pretensions of psychoanalysis altogether, confining their purview to the explication of those communications that are symbolically encoded, a psychoanalytic orientation often called "hermeneutic."

Not only have psychoanalytic hermeneuticists abandoned the Freudian ambition of establishing a science of mental functions, their aims also fail to include consideration of the influence of the preverbal stages of development on matters of clinical relevance. In this sense, they have disregarded Rapaport's insistence on the importance of the hierarchic organization of mental life, that is, that development must be understood as an epigenesis wherein the conditions of earlier phases are assimilated within those of later ones. Rubinstein (1976) was the first to point out that a psychology that accounts only for whatever is symbolically encoded cannot encompass the Freudian "unconscious." Although he did not have access to enough information about brain functions to propose a neurophysiological alternative to the old metapsychology and to hermeneuticism, he devised a purely hypothetical "proto-neurophysiology" (Rubinstein, 1974, 1976) in order to demonstrate that when we know the functioning of the brain sufficiently well, we shall be able to understand the control of behavior on the basis of that knowledge, without having to resort to hypothetical bridging concepts.[2]

---

[1] In later years, Loewald (1989) did make an effort to link these disparate theories by means of further speculative proposals; Kohut (1977) and Modell (1983), on the other hand, argued that psychoanalysis can afford to use several uncoordinated theoretical fragments. Although the point is defensible if we concern ourselves with clinical matters alone, such a policy would preclude the integration of psychoanalysis with psychology in general.

[2] In the meantime, the majority of theoreticians have preserved a biological orientation. Those who have adopted a hierarchical view of mental life (see Gedo and Goldberg, 1973; Gedo, 1979a, 1988) have striven to conceptualize the automatic repetition of patterned biological experiences from the preverbal era in later phases of development; others have continued to rely on the traditional vocabulary of metapsy-

More recently, an expanding cohort of scholars representing the next generation within psychoanalysis has mastered the flood of relevant information made available by the explosion of fruitful research in neurophysiology (see Hadley, 1985, 1989; Schwartz, 1987). Among them, Fred Levin (1991) has assumed the position of greatest scope, that of attempting to fulfill the program of Freud's 1895 "Project" and Rubinstein's work of the 1970s. Levin's effort is based on acceptance of the view that mental functions are hierarchically organized, that between the sensorimotor experience of the infant and the psychic organization of later life (characterized by the use of discursive symbols) are intermediate modes of adaptation, based on communication by means of concrete signals or presentational symbols. In retrospect, it might be said that, in the course of expectable human development, language "enfolds" preverbal experience. This process of learning naturally involves the momentous changes that constitute maturation of the nervous system.

Levin makes clear that the capacity of the brain to keep on changing, a capacity called "brain plasticity," underlies all subsequent learning, including the acquisition of those psychic functions that we usually understand by the term "analyzability." Another way to put this is that it has now been experimentally demonstrated that anything learned constitutes an anatomical change in the brain. It follows from this conclusion that the nervous system is best conceptualized as an organ of adaptation and that all psychological problems may fruitfully be viewed as learning disabilities. From this perspective, it is relevant to recall that the neural development of the prefrontal cortex is only "completed" around the age of 20, that is, when most people have learned to function as adults. If we accept the insight that adaptation is merely the dependent concomitant of neural control, it follows that it is mediated by the automatized decision-making processes of the brain—processes whereby information is used to produce goal-directed behavior. The operational "grammar" that characterizes these events in the brain is not yet understood—but this is the automatic functioning of neuronal systems that psychoanalysis has called "the unconscious."

As Freud did before him, Levin postulates that psyche and soma are isomorphic, that the mind/body dualism proposed by Descartes

---

chology while admitting that they understood this as a series of metaphors. Regrettably, this position is lacking in scientific justification.

(largely on religious grounds) is invalid, and that the vitalism that is hidden within contemporary mentalistic viewpoints serves to deny our animal heritage. He reviews man's evolutionary history, stressing that all mammalians have brains that give priority to auditory and visual stimuli (rather than olfactory ones), a development paralleled by the adaptively advantageous attachment between the young and their mothers. Among extant animals, only the apes seem to have the capacity to use a sign language, a capacity inborn in the human neonate and used from the cradle to the grave. Vocalization apparently first developed in the early hominids and eventually evolved into man's capacity to articulate over 40 phonemes – a protolanguage originally lacking in symbolic connotations. Verbalization presumably began relatively recently; yet the development of human languages tends to mask the fact that our communications actually consist of an integrated assembly of verbal and nonverbal modes. It is the developmental line of these communicative channels that we are able to study simultaneously from the psychological and the somatic vantage points. In other words, information processing may be conceptualized from the viewpoint of either neuroscience or of psychoanalysis.

Perhaps the most interesting of the findings about the maturation of the brain highlighted by Levin is that connections between the two cerebral hemispheres by means of the corpus callosum are generally established around the age of three and a half; thus the passage from the preoedipal to the oedipal period appears to be dependent on the ability to integrate the functions of the hemispheres – in the grossest of terms, those of primary and secondary processes. This reminds me of Daniel Stern's (1987) conjecture that entry into the psychic universe we call the Oedipus complex depends on the ability to construct a narrative. At any rate, Levin points out that intrapsychic conflict becomes possible when different functional units of the brain (most likely the hemispheres) are in fact connected to each other – a conclusion congruent with my view, derived from clinical observations, that in regressions to archaic modes of functioning, mutually incompatible attitudes may coexist without conflict (see Gedo, 1979a).

In agreement with Basch (1983), Levin views disavowal and repression as the means whereby thoughts are deprived of meaning by disconnecting affectivity from words and images. In this conception, repression is the process of blocking the input of the left cerebral hemisphere, while disavowal is the disconnection of right hemispheric input. Because of the advantages of communication by means of syntactically organized verbal codes, the left hemisphere becomes dominant (in right-handed persons) somewhere in the third year of life; this dominance facilitates gradual change toward the preferential use of repression as the typical defense, as the hierarchical model I proposed some years ago indicated (Gedo and Goldberg, 1973).

Although the human being's possession of a bicameral mind implies that learning takes place in terms of modules or subsystems that later undergo a process of integration (in 1973, Goldberg and I called these modules "nuclei of the self," and I later named the process of integrating them "self-organization" [Gedo, 1979a]), Levin makes clear that a core sense of self is formed well before the corpus callosum becomes fully functional. The weight of evidence suggests that the sense of self is originally a cerebellar function: the cerebellum forms maps of the body-in-space very early, so early, in fact, that it seems unlikely that the core sense of self could be experienced subjectively (i.e., consciously). Later these maps are duplicated in the central parietal cortex—I presume with accretions of remembered experience that transform these schemata into affectively charged motivational hierar-chies (see Emde, 1983). Levin is explicit in postulating that we possess a sequence of models of "self-in-the-world"; he conceives of transfer-ence as a strategy of the brain to resort to one of the earlier of these models as an adaptive experiment. Consequently, he also believes that the hierarchical model of mind I have developed should be regarded as a reflection of the hierarchic organization of the brain.

The expanding repertory of communicative channels available to the infant (gestural, sonic, verbal, and syntactical) produces the progres-sive changes in brain organization we have called psychological devel-opment. The acquisition of syntax reorganizes the brain most drasti-cally; Levin reminds us that this achievement is not contingent on the capacity for speech: verbal communication is not necessarily superior to the sign language of the deaf.[3] In any case, it is the frontal cortex that is implicated in providing an over-all organizer for behavior, and it is now known that this is the only area of the brain invariably implicated

---

[3] Fred Levin is one of the very few psychoanalysts capable of working in such a sign language; I believe his experience of working with deaf patients was an important influence in alerting him to the importance of understanding thought processes in neurophysiological terms.

in the use of language. Levin reports some experimental evidence from Japan that suggests that the specific physical (prosodic) qualities and syntactical rules of the natural language one learns may influence the nature of the operational grammar utilized by the brain.

Instead of my providing further details of Levin's review of the neuroscientific evidence he regards most relevant from a psychoanalytic vantage point, it may be more useful to consider whether his success in explicating all of the major clinical concepts of psychoanalysis in direct neurophysiological terms has implications beyond gaining impeccable scientific credentials for those concepts. My reading of this impressive effort to integrate two hitherto disparate realms of discourse is that it promises to alter profoundly both psychoanalytic theory *and* practice.

From the viewpoint of therapeutics, the cardinal implication of the new brain science is that treatment should be aimed at improving the information-processing skills available to the patient, a conclusion some authors have reached on clinical grounds (see Gardner, 1983, 1987a; Gedo, 1988, Epilogue). Another way to state the point is that the most important transaction in the process of analysis is the potential for the analysand to identify with the analyst's methods of data gathering and inference. Insofar as a therapeutic regression to conditions prevalent in childhood is a prerequisite for the emergence of the most relevant data, this requirement is probably promoted by the minimization of cerebellar input in the psychoanalytic situation. Analyzability may depend on the ability of higher centers to "manipulate" various cerebellar models of "self-in-the-world"; if these functions are not available in sufficient degree, the individual is able to respond to various contingencies only through enactments.

At the same time, the theoretical expectation behind the traditional technique of psychoanalysis, that of interpretation encoded in secondary-process terms, is revealed as ill grounded, for messages that rely entirely on discursive language are not likely to affect the more archaic layers of the hierarchy of schemata of the self. Levin advocates the analyst's use of metaphors in order to maximize communication with those levels of experience encoded in sensorimotor ways, in concrete signs, and in presentational symbols. His rationale is that metaphors are couched in linguistic symbols related to the various sensorimotor modalities. In cases where even such measures fail to establish adequate communication, it may be necessary to resort to methods that speak more directly to the right cerebral hemisphere, in right-handed persons, the seat of most of the dominant experience of the earliest years. Levin thus concurs with suggestions I have made in the past (Gedo, 1981b, chap. 11; 1984, chaps. 8 & 9) that communication by means of music and gesture may have to be employed – if you will, that the prosody of the analyst's speech may be as essential as its lexical content. He also points out that analysands may become blocked by neuronal gating within the brainstem; in these contingencies, internal processing (or the restoration of procedural memory) may be reestab- lished by means of "pump priming" – that is, the provision of crucial associations (preferably encoded in nonverbal ways) on the part of the analyst.[4]

It may be legitimate to summarize these therapeutic recommenda- tions as an endorsement of the need within psychoanalysis proper to extend the theory of technique to cover measures "beyond interpreta- tion" (see Gedo, 1979a). Levin believes that it is the soothing effect of the analytic procedures – as Modell (1976) put it, in Winnicott's termi- nology, analysis as a "holding environment," or its "empathic ambi- ance," as described by self psychologists – that reduces brainstem gat- ing, thereby giving access to the earliest cerebellar schemata of the mind/body self. An additional rationale for noninterpretive interven- tions in analysis is the need to influence "habits," that is, behaviors that remain repetitive because they are kept largely detached from cortical control, within the corticostriatal system. A propos, we seem to be on the threshold of a neurophysiological explanation for the repetition compulsion.

Hadley (1989) goes so far as to assert that the repetition compul- sion corresponds to the neurophysiological mechanism that underlies every type of motivation, namely, "the maintenance of familiarity of neural firing patterns" (p. 337). According to her thesis, this kind of repetition is "measured" by comparator mechanisms in the limbic system that signal the attainment of repetition by means of subjective "satisfactions" produced through neurochemical changes. These mech- anisms are not destined to produce repetition alone, for they are soon complemented by a second subsystem, "which supplies both positive and negative motivations depending on the outcomes of the matching

---

[4] In these contingencies, it is access to cerebellar models of the archaic self that is most likely to be at issue.

process and the addition of affect" (p. 337). Hadley calls this second process the pleasure-punishment principle.[5]

At any rate, it can no longer be maintained that intrapsychic conflict is an explanatory bedrock for all psychopathology. In the first place, much pathology is embedded in character as a consequence of neurocognitive difficulties; second, whenever conflicts remain chronically unresolved, this condition must be understood as a failure of information processing. In other words, this state in itself should also be classified as one form of neurocognitive deficit. We have come full circle, to a new appreciation – one that is better grounded in physiology – of Freud's concept of "actual neuroses." They are consequences of developmental lags, which we may now understand as failures of certain crucial maturational processes in the brain, usually as a result of prior disorganizing experiences.

The psychoanalyst as Biologist of the Mind must oppose the recurrent temptation to believe that "in the beginning was the Word." The infant develops a sophisticated repertory of semiological functions before it learns the verbal symbols provided by the caretakers. In psychoanalysis, as in all of life, the verbal and nonverbal realms are closely linked. Nonetheless, Levin (1991) believes, as I do, that therapeutic success is more fundamentally dependent on the nonverbal components of the transaction than on its lexical content. However, these conclusions must not be taken to mean that language competence is not essential – either for the analyst or for the analysand. On the contrary, it is the acquisition of language that provides the highest level of neural control in the prefrontal cortex; in this sense, cognitive functions are dependent on language. As Levin puts it, the operating system of the brain and the individual's native language share certain rules: memories are coded nonsensorially in a "machine language" the brain develops parallel to the acquisition of linguistic competence.[6]

---

[5] On the basis of these organizing mechanisms, the infant becomes able to pursue the various biological aims wired into the brain. According to Hadley, the aims thus far substantiated through brain research are exploratory (both assertive and aversive), sexual, sensual, and those of attachment and the regulation of physiological requirements.

[6] Levin makes note of the fact that the sign languages of the deaf seem to be closer to the basic linguistic code available to man than are languages using sonic symbols, as shown by the fact that it is easier to learn to use them interchangeably. In other words, the crucial aspect of language acquisition is *not* verbalization.

Nor would it be legitimate to jump to the conclusion that every instance of a syndrome that usually originates in the preoedipal (or even preverbal) era represents a direct homologue of archaic conditions. For example, Levin reports the finding that in sexual exhibitionists, the left cerebral hemisphere is unequipped–in the neurophysiological sense–to "police" the output of the right hemisphere. (Shades of the powerless rider on Freud's runaway horse!) Yet in the only two persons I have analyzed who suffered from this condition, the perversion supervened in adult life as a by-product of states of exultation. I have no doubt that in such states of excessive arousal the output of the right hemisphere escaped the usual controls, but the controls were more than adequate in ordinary circumstances. In other words, the syndrome was, in these two cases, not the sequel of a developmental lag but an outcome of very unusual circumstances that few people would be prepared to cope with on the basis of early experience. I cite this cautionary tale to emphasize that a neurophysiological approach to behavior need not lead to abandonment of the vast array of valid clinical knowledge psychoanalysis has accumulated in the course of the past century; better understanding of the archaic, biological roots of our humanity should lead instead to a more complex and nuanced view of the hierarchic adaptive possibilities of our behavioral repertory.

But emphasis should actually be placed on the obverse of this statement of reassurance to psychoanalysts long preoccupied with mental contents: the unfolding breakthrough toward a biology of mind promises soon to relegate hermeneutics to a secondary position in the analytic scheme of things and to focus primary attention on learning processes. The fruitful results of this coming revolution are incalculable.

CHAPTER 2

·——————————————·

Personality in Wonderland
The Nature/Nurture Controversy
Revisited

In his Presidential Address to the Society for Biological Psychiatry, Wagner Bridger (1989) asserted that the influence of the human (i.e., familial) milieu on the organization of personality has never been scientifically substantiated. By contrast, he offered an impressive array of published research demonstrating the decisive significance of genetically transmitted constitutional variables on the outcome of personality development. Although some of the studies cited are less relevant to the issue of "personality" as such than they are to the incidence of certain types of somatically caused psychopathology, Bridger's challenge deserves to be taken seriously, for the evidence needed to answer it is indeed difficult to find in some predigested form.

At the same time, it needs to be stated that such evidence is both copious and has long been available in a wide variety of publications – in effect, it may well be the ubiquitousness of the data that has led to the casualness about assuming their adequacy that Bridger decries. Perhaps the earliest sources of such data to have found their way into public print were observations about the personalities of severely neglected or so-called feral children. For instance, between 1802 and 1806, J.M.B. Itard published a series of careful and detailed reports about "the wild boy of Aveyron," a child found in the woods and for the subsequent seven years educated by Itard in an effort to acculturate him to human society. The very limited success of this therapeutic experiment would prove nothing about the etiology of the "wildness" of its subject, except for the fact that subsequent instances of this "natural experiment" have turned out in the same manner.

A striking and touching illustration in the recent literature is the work at the Hampstead Clinic in London with a number of very young children rescued from the death camp at Auschwitz (see esp. Ludowyk-Gyömröi, 1963). All these children were still extremely young at the time of liberation but had apparently been toilet-trained before separation from their mothers upon arrival at the camp. They owed their survival to the accident of having been chosen by various female guards as personal pets, presumably because of their attractiveness and docility. Although these children escaped physical abuse and malnutrition, eye-witness accounts suggest that they were treated as dogs or cats usually are, and not as members of the human community. Nonetheless, personal cleanliness (which was clearly a prerequisite for continued preferential status and survival) was maintained, and the development of language was not entirely precluded.

A number of these victims were subsequently raised at the Hampstead Nurseries, where psychotherapeutic assistance was also available to attempt to repair the damage to personality caused by the foregoing deprivations. These treatments provided unique opportunities for detailed longitudinal observations. To sum up the results of these studies in an extremely concise manner, they revealed arrestations of personality development at infantile levels, without obvious major damage to intellectual capacities. These results may perhaps be compared with the roughly analogous outcomes of Harlow's (1962) celebrated experiments with infant monkeys fed by wire-mesh simulacra of their mothers. You will recall that on reaching adulthood the experimental animals had difficulties in mating and in raising their young.

Stimulated by such findings, psychoanalytic researchers of the past generation have focused attention on the results of other varieties of "natural experiment" with a bearing on the influence of nurture on development. Probably the most cogent of these studies were those of Fraiberg and Freedman (1964) on children with congenital blindness. The researchers selected this population of the perceptually deprived because it had recently been learned that at least 25% of congenitally blind infants developed syndromes essentially indistinguishable from infantile autism. This figure is particularly startling because autism is an extremely rare condition in the general population; moreover, its incidence is no higher among the congenitally deaf than it is among perceptually unimpaired infants (Freedman, 1984). Congenital blindness may be caused by a wide variety of conditions, but the great majority of recent cases result from retrolental fibrous dysplasia, a complication suffered by a large number of prematurely born infants who manage to survive in incubators. In other words, most of the congenitally blind in the observational sample did not lose their sight from genetically transmitted causes.

Fraiberg and Freedman reasoned that the high incidence of autism among the congenitally blind points to the essential role of vision in establishing the kind of human attachments that permit the development of the human personality in its essentials. On the basis of these hypotheses, Fraiberg later devised elaborate protocols by means of which the caretakers of congenitally blind infants are able to maximize the perception of the human surround through alternate perceptual modalities. The use of such measures has proved to be highly successful in minimizing the risk of autism in this population. Incidentally, although her handicaps were not strictly speaking congenital, the celebrated case of Helen Keller long ago demonstrated that there is no substitute for the right kind of human transactions in promoting favorable personality development (see Dahl, 1965). Freedman (1984) cites another convincing instance of that kind, that of a normal infant raised for six and a half years in complete isolation by a totally aphasic mother (see Mason, 1932). The child had absolutely no language and was severely retarded in a number of other respects, but proper therapeutic intervention employing nonverbal communicative channels was successful in setting in motion progress in all areas.

I trust I have now given a sufficient sampling of the research data that prove that "average expectable" environmental conditions are an absolute prerequisite for satisfactory human personality development. I believe that the evidence is equally clear that certain constitutional variables are also decisive in this regard. Yet we must not forget that even in conditions as strongly influenced by genetic inheritance as are certain forms of schizophrenia, monozygotic twins are not always concordant for the disease. As Gottesman and Bertelsen (1989) have recently concluded, "discordance in identical twins may primarily be explained by the capacity of a schizophrenic genotype or diathesis to be unexpressed unless it is released by some kinds of environmental, including nonfamilial, stressors" (p. 867). As far as I know, we do not at present possess any evidence that would help to quantify the relative significance of familial versus nonfamilial and current versus predisposing vectors in this regard; our ignorance is even more marked about aspects of personality more subtle than is the occurrence of schizophrenia.

As one might expect in situations of such uncertainty, personality theorists have filled this vacuum of knowledge with a plethora of hypotheses. Even if we restrict the discussion to the domain of psychoanalysis and to theories that have found wide acceptance, these cover the gamut of possibilities from a predominant emphasis on the effects of nurture to a countervailing stress on the significance of constitutional variables. Probably the most ardent advocates of the primacy of nature are the followers of Melanie Klein (1984), who postulated that the decisive influence on personality is the individual's innate drive constitution. Klein barely paid lip service to the impact of the environment by conceding that the caretakers may be able to mitigate the effects of specific constitutional predispositions through unusual, not to say heroic, feats as educators. The other end of the spectrum is occupied by various advocates of theories of object relations. Perhaps the most interesting among these was Heinz Kohut (1971, 1978, 1984), who in turn paid lip service to the child's inborn propensities but insisted that appropriate parenting would generally–perhaps even always–be able to deal with these in a manner leading to a satisfactory outcome (see also chap. 11, this volume).

Sigmund Freud, aptly called a "biologist of the mind" by the historian of science Frank Sulloway (1979), maintained a middle-of-the-road position on this question. Perhaps because such a position is the most complex among the alternatives, it is probably true that it has lost support in favor of its reductionist competitors–thus lending some degree of plausibility to Bridger's (1989) charge that the discipline overestimates the enduring influence of familial transactions. But my own clinical observations have led me to formulate the problem from a completely different vantage point: I do not see the issue in quantitative terms, as the outcome of so much constitutional influence mediated by some quantum of countervailing nurture; on the contrary, for me the crux of the matter is the specific impact of particular environmental influences on the biological predispositions of the individual.

My clinical experience as a psychoanalyst over the last 30 years has led me to progressively greater wonder about the complexities of these transactions. Let me provide a brief illustration of these bewildering tangles of causation. Some years ago I performed an analysis for an academician in early middle age who consulted me because of a marital crisis that was the culmination of many years of tempestuous difficulties with women (see Gedo, 1988, chap. 1). In temperament my patient was utterly different from other members of his family. His father was a reserved, obsessional, prudent, and tenacious professional man; his mother, equally successful in a different domain, was charismatic, refined, snobbish, generous, and loyal. His only sibling, a younger brother, had some combination of the characteristics of both parents. In contrast, my patient was passionate, bold, unreasonable, childlike, inconsistent, and gullible.

It did not take us long to grasp that some of these qualities, as well as the adaptive difficulties with women who became close to him, constituted the perpetuation of a quasi-symbiotic pattern of living that he and his mother had worked out quite early in his childhood, apparently in response to his severe and unfavorable emotional reaction to the birth of his brother and to a subsequent separation from mother necessitated by a lengthy illness on her part. In many ways, the boy became the very opposite of his father, or, if you will, the ideal partner of a woman like his mother. She had been enormously gratified, albeit her pleasure was laden with guilt, by her brilliant son's manifest emotional need for her continuing overinvolvement with him. One would have thought that the case was a clear instance of the primacy of environmental factors in character formation – an object lesson of how to turn a boy into a modern-day Oedipus. But this impression was almost entirely illusory.

We gradually came to appreciate that the patient's mother had chosen the best of the alternatives available to her when she forged the bonds with him that, in adult life, appeared to constitute his personality disorder. To put this somewhat differently, as her contemporary diaries revealed, she was quite aware that something was radically amiss with her older son some time before the younger one was born, and she lent herself to his emotional demands because the alternative was to let him lapse into states of despair and exhaustion. To make a long story short enough for our purposes here, the child had suffered from infantile eczema since shortly after birth, and this untreatable condition had led to severe pruritus, dangerous scratching, attempted coercive countermeasures, storms of rage, and so on. In other words, the infant was repeatedly traumatized, and it was to safeguard him as much as possible from the recurrence of these states that his mother initiated the overinvolvement between them. It would seem, then, that in the final analysis, the personality disorder was based primarily on a constitutional abnormality that severely skewed the infant's subjective experience in the direction of discomforts only partially mitigated by the best of nurture. We can only speculate what the fate of this person would have been if his parents had been less conscientious and devoted, but I feel confident that their excellence as caretakers saved this man from more severe psychopathology.

By the same token, certain constitutionally based assets of the child may permit acceptable adaptive solutions to be reached in stressful circumstances that would utterly defeat a person who does not possess that special endowment. Perhaps the unusual docility of the handful of children who survived Auschwitz may have constituted a predisposition of this kind. I can certainly offer a parallel example from my analytic practice. The youngest of six children of a paranoid schizophrenic mother, my patient had grown up to be a moderately accomplished professional person but generally avoided intimate relations with women. He sought analysis because he felt that some of his characterological attributes impaired his work performance. This complaint was justified, because he was simultaneously too passive— unable to take appropriate initiatives in the manner desired in his profession—and too rebellious, albeit in a covert fashion.

It should be noted that the patient's mother became psychotic a few years before he was born. She was hospitalized at the time for a relatively brief period and thereafter was cared for at home, although she never had a real remission. The three oldest children were exposed to her illness for relatively brief periods; each of them was sent off to boarding school as early as possible. Only the patient lived his entire childhood in the atmosphere of a poorly run madhouse. Remarkably, he was the only member of the family who never had trouble with the psychotic mother, who made several homicidal attacks on other family members, including some of the children. The price of my patient's immunity from his mother's murderous hostility was his willingness to comply with her demands, even when these were delusional. The two siblings closest to him in age, both girls, were the principal victims; instead of complying with their mother's tyranny, they both appear to have identified with her as an aggressor (often submitting their younger brother, who was the tyrant's ally and acolyte, to considerable abuse). It is scarcely surprising that these sisters grew up to be much more impaired psychologically than did my patient: they were much more eccentric, albeit less solitary than their brother. (Interestingly, among the children, only two older brothers had families of their own; although both had stable marriages, one child in each family subsequently became psychotic.)

Of course, I have no right to claim that my patient's docility was inherited, as was the schizophrenic genotype in his mother's family. Nonetheless, in my opinion, this aspect of my patient's character was indeed genetically transmitted. The evidence on which I base my judgment came to light in the course of a psychoanalysis that involved over 1,500 "hours" of observations. The relevant data involved countless episodes of "automatic obedience"—complex behaviors demonstrating a suspension of the patient's customary habits and powers of judgment in favor of an entirely thoughtless, instantaneous, and disastrous compliance with the requirements of someone else. Clearly, this pattern of behavior regulation marked a regression to the symbiotic mode that had made it possible for this man to live in peace with his dangerous mother, and its periodic recurrence in the course of treatment was, in one sense, simply a manifestation of an archaic transference, what some analysts call a state of "merger." But these relatively infrequent events occurred against the background of a steady state of equally automatic negativism, just as thoughtless and instantaneous as its compliant counterpart, and *this* mode of adaptation did not constitute an iatrogenic artefact. On the contrary, it was the lifelong personality attribute that ultimately led this man to seek psychoanalytic assistance. In my judgment, the patient's capacity to continue to employ a mode of behavior regulation that short-circuits the cortical processing characteristic of human functioning even in the first half of the second year of life suggests that he was not unaffected by the constitutional handicaps so much clearer in a number of others in his family.

Be that as it may, in other instances, the specific attribute that may

save a child from potential disaster is very clearly an inherited endowment. I have had the privilege, over the years, of analyzing an unusual
number of creative individuals (see Gedo, 1983). My overall impression is that the opportunity to make use of a great talent permits these
people to master contingencies, particularly in the realm of self-esteem
regulation, that tend to crush more ordinary persons. I do not mean
simply that in adult life scientific or artistic accomplishment will
compensate one for a variety of other troubles, although that statement
is evidently correct. Beyond that, I have found that many of these
people begin their creative careers in childhood by arriving at original
conceptions of the confusing life situations in which they find themselves. For example, one of my patients was able to save herself from
being sucked into a folie-à-deux with her dotty mother by coming to
the solitary realization, around the age of two and a half, that the
mother was *delusional* in her overestimation of the child. Most of us
would be incapable of that feat at any age!

In the confusing welter of biological and environmental circumstances that constitutes a life, what seems to add up to the enduring
organismic characteristics we call "personality" are guiding memories
of past experience, including (of course) the outcomes of particular
adaptive solutions attempted. From this perspective, the nature/nurture
controversy begins to sound absurd, for every adaptive challenge draws
on our biological resources, as amplified by our training, in a given
human (and social) context. Our biological equipment is continuously
changing, for better or for worse, and the direction and extent of these
changes is to a very large degree determined by environmental input.
Even at the somatic level (to leave behavior regulation aside for a
moment), human encounters are just as significant in determining such
changes as are encounters with microorganisms, toxins, or pharmacological agents. In other words, biology is conceivable only within an
environmental context, and nurture means nothing more than the
preprogrammed biological changes effected over time in a sequence of
milieux. Both terms refer to the same seamless, dynamic process and
merely designate aspects of that process, arbitrarily torn out of context
by the observer.

To make this crucial point as clear as possible, I should like to offer
still another example taken from analytic practice. This patient was
also the youngest of a large family; his mother was more psychopathic
than psychotic, but part of her delinquency was manifest in her virtual

abandonment of this runt in her litter to the inconsistent mercies of his older siblings. As far as inherited characteristics go, this family was also afflicted with severe stigmata: several brothers had reversible psychotic episodes at various stages of life, and one of them committed suicide in the course of an agitated depression in middle age. My patient developed a sadistic perversion that led him, in late adolescence, to the decision to avoid sexual relations altogether, and he lived an isolated existence devoted to reasonably successful professional pursuits. It was this bleak, virtually solipsistic mode of adaptation that led him repeatedly to seek psychological assistance.

In his numerous periods of psychotherapy or psychoanalysis, with me as well as with several others, he sought to establish a sadomasochistic equilibrium that would echo the emotional tone of his close childhood bond with a brother two years older than he who had treated him in a manner that any outside observer would have characterized as child abuse. Of course, from the patient's subjective viewpoint, masochistic submission to abuse constituted the only expectable emotional closeness in life. It would not be inaccurate to say that a sadomasochistic relationship served this man as an effective home remedy for the anaclitic depression that was ever threatening to swamp him. The propensity for depression is probably inherited – the genotype is more than likely activated into the phenotype by the atrocious child-rearing practices of a similarly afflicted parent (see chap. 6, this volume). The characterological defenses against the recurrence of "disorder and early sorrow" seem to be determined by adventitious environmental factors that could doubtless be further broken down to their own genetically determined anlagen.

I do not wish to burden the reader with unnecessary clinical details here. Perhaps it will suffice simply to add that the single specific aspect of "nurture" I learned about in this case that had the greatest impact on the development of personality was the mother's practice of soothing the slightest sign of distress in her baby by sticking a bottle of sugared water in his mouth. Needless to say, he became a voracious food addict and a grossly obese adult. And yet – and yet! – almost every member of this family seemed to be highly "nervous" throughout life: obsessional worry-warts, timid to a fault. Could it be that the mother's ordinary caretaking efforts could not satisfy this child because his constitutional needs were unusually great? But to ask this question merely underscores the senselessness of the nature/nurture controversy: in the last analysis, it is the infant's subjective experience that rules its subsequent destiny, and that experience is always, of necessity, the product of biological givens evolving under the impact of a specific ecology. Students of human behavior would do well to emulate zoologists, who have transcended the sterility of this controversy, fueled by epistemological naiveté, by forging the discipline of ethology.

After all, we know that the personality of every duckling is forever altered by the nature of the creature upon which it is imprinted, but nobody would dream of conceiving that the attainment of duck-hood is a consequence of some disembodied process named "nurture."

II

Biology and Clinical Syndromes

CHAPTER 3

· ———————————— ·

The Hierarchical Model of
Mental Functioning

A PERSONAL HISTORY

In the 1950's, when I first turned to the serious study of psycho-analysis, the theoretical revolution Freud brought to the discipline through his great conceptual works of the 1920s (Freud, 1920, 1923, 1926) had occurred within the professional lifetimes of my teachers. Indeed, less time had elapsed since the promulgation of this "structural theory" (summed up in Freud's "tripartite" model of the mind) than I have spent in our professional domain since those years of apprentice-ship. From the vantage point of 1990, it may be difficult to realize that in the years following the second world war the structural theory was still encountering some conservative resistance on the part of survivors of a previous generation, brought up in the intoxicating atmosphere of early psychoanalysis and its conceptual simplicities. The most progres-sive theoretical work on the contemporary scene was that of Hartmann and his collaborators (Hartmann, 1939, 1964; Hartmann, Kris, and Loewenstein, 1964), then regarded as bold revisionists.

In the pluralistic ambience of 1990, my generation looks back on the unthinking enthusiasm that characterized our entry into psycho-analysis with a mixture of embarrassment and wry amusement. Therapeutic optimism was at its height – be it in experimentation with brief therapy (Alexander and French, 1946; Alexander, 1956), with the hospital treatment of psychotic patients (Fromm-Reichmann, 1950; Sullivan, 1940, 1956), or with broadening the scope of psychoanalysis proper to groups of patients Freud regarded as unanalyzable (see M. Klein, 1984). The triumphant incursions of psychoanalysts into American psychiatry encouraged the application of an accepted theoretical system to the challenge of contiguous fields, such as psychosomatic medicine or in-patient treatment, without too much inquiry into the adequacy of that conceptual schema.

Yet the pioneers who conducted these "colonial ventures" (Freud's description of C.G. Jung's analogous activities ca. 1912) had a disquieting tendency to break the psychoanalytic consensus by systematizing their findings within theoretical frameworks that could not be reconciled with any of Freud's schemata. Within the quasi-religious atmosphere that then prevailed, such proposals led to numerous schisms and secessions and considerable dissension within organized psychoanalysis. Elsewhere, I (Gedo, 1986), have attempted to explore the dynamics of such disputes, using among my illustrative cases the controversies aroused by the work of Ferenczi in the 1920s and 30s, and that of Melanie Klein in the 40s and 50s. It would have been just as cogent to use the example of the American interpersonal school that grew out of the work of Harry Stack Sullivan or the object relations theories put forward by the British "middle group," which tried to remain neutral in the civil war between Freudian traditionalists and Kleinian radicals (see Fairbairn, 1954; Winnicott, 1958).

In Chicago, where Alexander led the exciting enterprise of developing alternative models of psychoanalytic therapy and Roy Grinker established a first-rate psychoanalytic hospital within a comprehensive medical center, but the Institute for Psychoanalysis gave my cohort of candidates an impeccably traditional education, I found it impossible to dismiss any of the competing points of view. Although I was baffled about how some of these might be reconciled, I found all of them to be reductionistic, including the most sophisticated efforts to conceptualize the gamut of psychoanalytic findings under the aegis of the structural theory (Arlow and Brenner, 1964). I became convinced that lasting controversies within psychoanalysis are caused by seemingly reasonable conclusions, based on unrepresentative population samples and adhered to with excessive rigidity. This view was reinforced by the major scholarly project I undertook in the mid-1960s, a thorough review of Ferenczi's total contribution (Gedo, 1967; commissioned by *Psyche* on the occasion of the reissue of Ferenczi's four-volume corpus of writings in German).

Serendipitously, the next significant assignment that came my way was a request from the *Psychoanalytic Quarterly* to assess the *Collected Papers* of David Rapaport (1967) in some detail. I took this responsibility most seriously (see Gedo, 1973; 1986, chap. 5), for I regarded Rapaport to have been the only psychoanalytic author of the postwar era who approached the subject matter of our discipline in an ecumenical spirit. In his monograph of 1960, Rapaport had made "a systematizing attempt" to map out the conceptual terrain of psycho-analysis and the nature of the evidence on which those concepts were based. I believed his effort had been largely successful. In order to make it so, however, Rapaport was forced to keep to a level of abstraction so far removed from clinical observations that it remained extremely difficult to correlate the theories competing for our attention with his general propositions.

At any rate, I decided to approach the project for the *Quarterly* by studying all of Rapaport's psychoanalytic writings in the sequence of their publication – the methodology I had already used for my work on Ferenczi. This effort brought to my attention Rapaport's scholarly compilation of 1951, *The Organization and Pathology of Thought,* where I encountered Rapaport's insistence that developmental psychology must be understood as an epigenetic sequence organized in a hierar-chical manner – a concept already employed by Piaget in his work on the development of cognition (summarized in Piaget, 1971) and, much earlier, by Hughlings Jackson (1884) in his description of brain func-tioning. It occurred to me that the various parts of the psychoanalytic elephant described by our quarreling sages might well be capable of correlation into an internally consistent schema by being arranged in a *developmental* sequence. And the manner in which such a sequence could be arranged hierarchically was suggested to me by the models em-ployed in Erikson's 1959 monograph, *Identity and the Life Cycle,* a work that was lent its conceptual rigor through an introductory essay pro-vided by Rapaport![1]

When I decided to embark on this theoretical exploration, in the

---

[1] Recently, Grossman (in press) has demonstrated that the concept of hierarchically structured subsets of mental organization was implicit in Freud's theorizing all along. This insight was not consciously available to me until I read Grossman's essay.

late 1960s, I had barely transcended the status of a psychoanalytic beginner, and the task of writing a book of any kind seemed overwhelming to me, unless I could find a collaborator. Consequently, I shared my idea with a colleague, Arnold Goldberg, whose critical intelligence and epistemological sophistication promised to complement my assets and limitations in the service of this project. Goldberg approved of my idea and agreed to coauthor the book. In retrospect, his agreement with my viewpoint may have been highly provisional, for he has never written about these matters again, and his subsequent writings have espoused and promoted self psychology–a school of thought that I have come to view as antithetical to an ecumenical enterprise (see chap. 11, this volume). Goldberg and I parted company shortly after *Models of the Mind* (Gedo and Goldberg, 1973) was published because I disagreed with the views Kohut began to share with us around 1974.

To be sure, while we were writing *Models of the Mind*, self psychology did not yet exist, and my coauthor and I were about equally interested in and influenced by the work of our preeminent teacher, Heinz Kohut. At the time we started research for our book, Kohut had published three major papers (1959, 1966, 1968) that seemed to open the door to the understanding and rational psychoanalytic treatment of various syndromes that I later proposed to name "archaic" (Gedo, 1977a). In my view (see Gedo, 1981b, Section II; 1986, chaps. 7 & 8), Kohut's work through 1972–that is, the preliminary papers mentioned, his 1971 book, and his 1972 paper on aggression–offered a provisional and reasonable alternative to the less than satisfactory proposals of predecessors such as Ferenczi and Melanie Klein concerning the problems of the archaic psyche. Consequently, in *Models of the Mind*, we concentrated on Kohut's earlier formulations about these matters to the neglect of various alternatives. Today, it may be difficult to believe that in following this option we earned the concurrence of Anna Freud, who was kind enough to read our earliest drafts.

TOWARD A DEVELOPMENTAL PSYCHOANALYSIS

The conceptual tool long available to psychoanalysis to lend order to its propositions concerning the maturation of personality is that of "developmental lines" (see Freud, 1905a; Ferenczi, 1913; A. Freud,

1965). The most familiar of these sequences is the succession of libidinal phases (see Abraham, 1924): oral, anal, phallic, and so forth. The lines of development are to be understood as listings describing successive conditions that *predominate* within defined spans of time. In other words, the advent of the anal phase must not be conceptualized as a cessation of orality; it only signals a shift of emphasis from one libidinal zone to another. Alerted to the theoretical flexibility afforded by this concept through the then recent work of Anna Freud (1965), *Normality and Pathology in Childhood*, I determined to attempt to coordinate as many as possible of the lines of development widely regarded as significant in terms of adaptation, to form one coherent schema.

Goldberg and I were pleasantly surprised to find that most psychoanalytic authors had postulated five significant phases for whichever lines of development they happened to be outlining. When, on occasion, someone proposed a sequence of more than five phases (as Abraham tried to do for libidinal development in 1924), common usage tended to elide some of them. There seemed to be consensus that the libidinal phases that matter are those named oral, anal, phallic, oedipal, and postoedipal. (I here use this most familiar of examples, although Goldberg and I decided not to include this line of development in our schema, because we felt that libidinal interests are so ubiquitous and changeable that they cannot be used for diagnostic purposes.) At any rate, it was the nature of much of the preexisting literature that dictated our choice of a five-phase schema. Although we stressed that one could make only an arbitrary decision in this regard, we also found this number of variables to be most convenient in terms of an appropriate balance between differentiating cogent phasic units and avoiding an unmanageable complexity.

In *Models of the Mind*, the developmental lines chosen for the effort of correlation were those of the most prominent (or "typical") situations of danger, of the predominant (or "typical") mechanisms of defense used to deal with dangers, of the expectable nature of the prevailing object relationships, of reality testing, and of the state of "narcissism." We leaned on the correlation previously noted by Modell (1968) between the secure achievement of reality testing and viewing objects as whole and differentiated from the self. It also became apparent that, for phases that follow the attainment of these maturational steps, these developmental lines had been but poorly elaborated, so that so-called object relations theories would prove to be no more

serviceable as a basic framework for psychoanalytic psychology than
was the libido theory. To put this another way, drive theories and
object relations theories, which had never been properly reconciled,
seemed to be applicable in circumstances referable to different phases of
the developmental sequence.

Despite the foregoing exception to a neat five-phase sequence for
all these lines of development, we found that existent theories postulated essentially contemporaneous transitions from each earlier phase
within the lines to a later one. We decided to call these transitional eras
"nodal points." In other words, we found that the developmental
hypotheses of psychoanalysis appeared to posit that certain reasonably
well-defined phases of maturation are organized into characteristic
modes of functioning (to which we simply gave numerical designa-
tions, I through V). We hypothesized, in turn, that these modes of
organization become available as a hierarchically arranged set of potentialities, as each of them is added to the behavioral repertory in the
course of development. (The nodal events at these points of transition
are the acquisition of a series of essential psychological structures, such
as consolidation of a cohesive self-organization or the formation of a
repression barrier.) We believed that this conceptualization amounted
to the introduction of systems theory into psychoanalytic discourse.

It proved to be relatively easy to demonstrate that each of the five
modes of mental functioning we had discerned as implicit features of
existing psychoanalytic hypotheses about development corresponds to
one of the (competing) clinical theories then extant in the psychoanalytic arena. Modes V and IV are explicated by Freud's topographic
theory of 1900 and his structural theory of 1923, respectively; modes
III and II by theories of object relations dealing with whole objects and
part objects; and mode I by the hypotheses about primitive mentation
also put forward by Freud (1900) in *The Interpretation of Dreams*. Freud had
drawn graphic "models of the mind" to represent the three theories he
had devised: the topographic model, the tripartite model, and that of
the reflex arc; my coauthor and I made a somewhat feeble effort to
draw models representing the more recent theories of object relations.
Thus each mode within the overall hierarchy of psychic functioning
could still be conceptualized in terms of theories and models previously
introduced, but we offered a novel articulation of these conceptual
fragments into an integrated whole we called the "hierarchical model."

As this model is drawn, it forms a layered edifice or grid of the functional modes; the passage of time is represented by movement from left to right that adds successive new modes to the repertory, drawn one on top of the other. (Figure 1 represents a version of the model elaborated in Gedo, 1988.) Thus the fully differentiated psyche consists of a hierarchy of five modes; functional regression is represented by downward movement from more mature to more primitive alternatives—progress by ascent in the opposite direction. We made provision for the possibility of the regression-proof maturation of specific functions by permitting them to be represented as leaving the area of the grid (upward) into an implied area of "secondary autonomy" (Hartmann, 1939). This possibility is made more explicit in the 1988 version of the model shown here.

The clinical significance of this hierarchic view of development

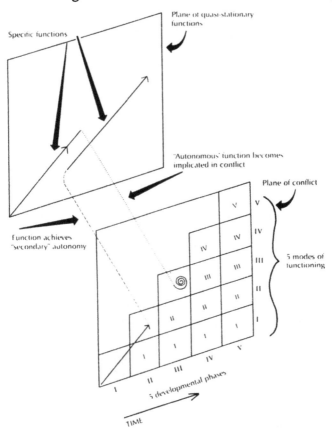

Figure 1. The hierarchical model of mental functioning

was spelled out in both nosological and therapeutic terms. The schema views clinical syndromes not as disease entities but as adaptive responses to particular environmental demands, responses that consist of selecting that mode from the repertory of functional alternatives which promises to attain as many of the person's goals, in conformity with his or her ideals, as possible under the circumstances. Although everyone tends to make use of all of the functional modes in the repertory, in a maximally flexible manner, as dictated by rapidly shifting requirements, predominant use of one or another mode will lend the personality a more or less archaic flavor that corresponds to one of the major diagnostic categories of psychopathology. In other words, expectable adult functioning implies a predominance of mode V; if mode IV is the one selected most of the time, personality functioning is in the "neurotic" realm; if mode III is predominant, the adaptation will have the characteristics of "narcissistic" disturbances; the prevalence of mode II is the hallmark of "psychotic" adjustment, and that of mode I betokens the advent of a traumatic state. If, on the other hand, one or more of the more advanced modes are simply unavailable to an individual, this failure to mature may be conceived as an *arrest* of development. The situational regressive swings that often punctuate such cases yield the symptomatic picture often termed "borderline."

To avoid confusion with a putative schema of disease entities, it is actually preferable to lay stress on the differing principles of behavior regulation prevalent in each mode. Thus mode I is ruled by the principle of (avoidance of) unpleasure, mode II by that of organismic integration, mode III by the pleasure principle, mode IV by that of reality; for mode V I proposed a principle of creativity. (In 1983, I explored this mode in my monograph, *Portraits of the Artist: Psychoanalysis of Creativity and Its Vicissitudes.*)

As corollaries of the clusters of maladaptation, there are different therapeutic requirements at each level of regression from expectable adult functioning, wherein introspection is sufficient to achieve conflict resolution. The modality of treatment appropriate to deal with the unconscious intrapsychic conflicts characteristic of mode IV is the traditional interpretive technique of psychoanalysis. In states of deeper regression, measures "beyond interpretation" are required—a phrase I selected as the title of my 1979(a) book, in which I tried to spell out these noninterpretive techniques. In *Models of the Mind*, Goldberg and I

(1973) contented ourselves with listing these modalities of treatment: regression to mode III necessitates dealing with a variety of (narcissistic) illusions by means of nontraumatic (i.e., "optimal") disillusionment; the disorganization characteristic of mode II must be remedied through measures promoting reintegration, that is, "unification" of the total personality; the disturbances of tension regulation encountered in mode I require techniques of "pacification." In a psychoanalytic context, these measures are considered to be the "parameters" of technique Eissler (1953) advocated in cases of impaired ego functioning. In nonanalytic therapies, the same measures may constitute the principal tools of relatively brief treatment programs (see Gustafson, 1984, 1986).

CLINICAL EXPERIENCE WITH THE HIERARCHICAL MODEL

For most of the decade from 1969 to 1978, I was deeply immersed in the clinical practice of psychoanalysis, conducted mostly on a schedule of five sessions per week–a clinical laboratory where I attempted to put the propositions put forward in *Models of the Mind* to a preliminary clinical trial. I was doubly determined to test my ideas because the book, despite uniformly favorable reviews, was everywhere received as a clever conceptual exercise without practical significance. From my vantage point, by contrast, these conceptual clarifications seemed immensely helpful in pinpointing when and why parametric interventions should be resorted to in psychoanalytic work. Although any decrease of an analyst's bewilderment is bound to increase his or her effectiveness and therefore cannot serve as evidence for the validity of the hypotheses that produced it, the magnitude of the improvement in my therapeutic results encouraged me to hope that I had found an effective conceptual tool. I have reported these promising results on more than one occasion (Gedo, 1979b; 1984, chap. 2; see also chap. 10, this volume) and have also published extensive case reports illustrating my analytic techniques (Gedo, 1979a, chaps. 4, 6, and 8; and 1984, chaps 4 and 5 contain the most detailed presentations of individual cases).

In the course of these clinical experiments, I gradually became convinced that the hierarchical model could be greatly improved through more careful consideration of certain issues within psychoanalytic psychology that Goldberg and I had consciously decided not to address in *Models of the Mind*. Specifically, we had avoided the controversy that was gathering steam in the late 1960s about the epistemological status of Freud's metapsychology – a clash of opinions that was to produce a cluster of important theoretical statements during the next decade (see G. Klein, 1976; Schafer, 1976; Gill and Holzman, 1976; Rosenblatt and Thickstun, 1977). We took cognizance of this unresolved issue by constructing our model in such a way that its validity and usefulness would remain unimpaired no matter how the metapsychological controversy was eventually decided; we made no reference to the concept of psychic energy and tried, as much as possible, to take for granted that psychoanalytic psychology is built around a tenable theory of motivation. (The major exception to this policy was our inclusion of the line of development of "narcissism" within the schema. It is true that, unlike Kohut in his works prior to 1973, my coauthor and I did not use this term in its narrower – and technically more correct! – sense of denoting vicissitudes of narcissistic libido; by the same token, however, we had covertly distorted its original meaning.)

When, in the early 1970s, Kohut was persuaded by some of his followers (notably Goldberg and Michael Basch) to abandon his adherence to traditional metapsychology – or, if you will, to give up his effort to assume the mantle of Heinz Hartmann as the savior of the paradigm of psychic energy – much of the controversy about that tradition became confused with the entirely separate issue of the adequacy of the system Kohut (1977, 1984) proposed to substitute for it. To prevent my own work from being wrongly subsumed within this new controversy, I published a series of papers clarifying my position vis-à-vis Kohut's clinical findings and theoretical propositions (Gedo, 1975b; 1977b; 1980; see also Gedo, 1986, chaps. 7 & 8; chap. 11, this volume). The crux of the matter was that, seduced by my conviction that Kohut had accurately pinpointed a number of hitherto neglected transference constellations, I had reached a false agreement with him on his theoretical propositions. To be more precise, when Kohut began to write about a "psychology of the self," I mistakenly assumed that he was adumbrating a theory focused on the organization of the total personality, whereas (as the subsequent history of self psychology has made clear) he actually had in mind an object relations theory dealing only with what he called "self–selfobject relations"–a matter that in the hierarchical model is dealt with in terms of our mode II. When, in *Models of the Mind,* I insisted on summarizing Kohut's work under the heading of an "emerging psychology of the self," I was predicting not the course of his future work (despite his appropriation of that name for it) but that of my own.

To return to the major theoretical debate of the 1970s, my own convictions were shaped by numerous personal encounters with one of the leading revisionists, George Klein, who encouraged me to tackle the project that resulted in *Models of the Mind.* He rightly saw it as a potential demonstration of the *irrelevance* of traditional metapsychology for the clinical theories in actual use. By the time I got the privilege of reviewing Klein's posthumous book (Gedo, 1977b) in tandem with the monograph Gill and Holzman (1976) edited in his memory, I greeted these revolutionary works by comparing them to the fall of the Bastille, although I did not endorse their specific programs for a New Regime–in Klein's case largely because it was left unfinished at his death. In the work of other hermeneuticists, I was dissatisfied by total neglect of the preverbal phases of development (i.e., the failure to adopt a hierarchical model) as well as the adoption of this newly fashionable epistemology. (For a critique of hermeneutics as a psychoanalytic methodology, see Gedo, 1986, chap. 13.)

Unlike Schafer (1976) (or the later Kohut, 1984), I remain committed to psychoanalysis as a discipline grounded in biology. Indeed, the hierarchical model embraces an initial phase of postnatal existence wherein behavior regulation is governed entirely by inborn neurophysiological mechanisms that operate automatically (i.e., without prior learning through deliberate instruction or the interposition of symbolic systems). As I wrote in the Preface to *Beyond Interpretation* (1979a),

> The central concept around which my tentative revision of psychoanalytic psychology is built is that of human personality as a hierarchy of personal aims. The infant's biological needs constitute the earliest of these goals; by the end of the second year of life, these have been supplemented by a variety of subjective wishes; the entire hierarchy, in both conscious and unconscious aspects, will form the person's primary identity, or, as I would prefer to call it, the "self-

organization." The formation of the self-organization and its later transformations, especially through the acquisition of systems of values, should be viewed in epigenetic terms as the core of personality development [p. xi].

Given these convictions, it became necessary to reconsider the details of the hierarchical model of 1973. As the motto of my renewed effort, I chose Danton's revolutionary slogan, *"Toujours de l'audace!"*

THE HIERARCHICAL MODEL REVISED

In *Beyond Interpretation*, I (1979a) began to advocate abandonment of the traditional theories and models of psychoanalysis in favor of the hierarchical schema, now understood as the delineation of the epigenesis of self-organization, that is, of the hierarchic arrangements of the sum of personal goals. This change permits us, at the same time, to dispense with the entire set of metaphors Freud borrowed from 19th-century physics: apparatus, forces, and energies can be replaced with concepts that refer to the actual functions performed by the brain as an information-processing organ. I credited Lichtenstein (1964, 1965) with being the first to propose a conception of self, which he called a "primary identity," as the organizer of subsequent psychic life. This view is utterly different from that of self as a content of the mind (i.e., merely a representation). My conception of self as a mental structure implies a hierarchy of potentials for action, ipso facto laden with affect and extending beyond the realm of subjective intentionality into a nonexperiential one involving constitutionally given, physiological capacities for satisfying organismic needs.[2] Incidentally, these notions support the contention of Rubinstein (1976) that when psychoanalysis postulates a realm of unconscious mental life, it is focused on matters in part beyond the reach of subjectivity and introspection.

The self-organization is gradually formed in the course of phases I and II of development; when discrete personal goals have been ordered within a unified hierarchy of motivations, this achievement may be

---

[2] I first presented the concept of self-as-structure in May 1975 at the Panel on "New Horizons in Metapsychology" of the American Psychoanalytic Association (Panel, 1976).

called the attainment of a cohesive self. That is to say, the principal task of phase II is the achievement of motivational integration, and the "typical" problem encountered whenever there is regression into mode II is the disruption of self-cohesion. Cohesiveness means the relatively stable structuring of goals and values into potentials for action, a process we might also call "self-definition." Following this achievement (in mode III), it becomes possible to view behavior as regulated by the pleasure principle, that is, in terms of seeking satisfactions on the basis of purposeful choices. When Freud (1920) postulated a realm of behavior "beyond the pleasure principle," he was referring to the derivatives of what I call modes I and II, which manifest themselves in adulthood as an overriding, unverbalizable need to restore self-cohesion, at whatever cost. Hence Freud was fully justified in attributing these behaviors to a "repetition compulsion."

The second major revision of the hierarchical model I offered in 1979 concerned phase I in development and consisted in an effort to substitute more plausible hypotheses for Freud's untenable suggestion that the essential challenge of mentation in the infant is the discharge of quanta of psychic energy. In this regard, I leaned on the prior work of Basch (1975a, b, c; 1976a, b, c), who postulated that the principal issue of this phase is the ordering of experience (i.e., novel stimuli); through the continuous monitoring of environmental signals, stable representations of patterned transactions with the milieu are formed. This process is facilitated by a system of communication with the caretakers through preprogrammed patterns of expressive signals that accompany affective reactions.

In these terms, the traditional notion that the newborn's behavior is regulated in accordance with the need to avoid unpleasure should be understood as the need to forestall progressive disorganization (trauma). Thus, the characteristics of mode I can best be described in terms of a model we might call "sensorimotor," because it portrays behavior that does not involve the operation of the cerebral cortex.

The last revision in the model necessitated by repudiation of the concept of psychic energy concerned the line of development of "narcissism," which is rendered hollow by such a deformation of drive theory. In its place, I suggested considering (in parallel with the development of object relations) the evolution of attitudes about one's own person—from the earliest phases in which there is no self-awareness, through various illusory, wish-fulfilling views of oneself, to the attainment of realistic self-esteem.[3] Clearly, the maturation of these functions depends on the development of more precise perception and cognition; consequently, I also suggested that the developmental line of reality testing might preferably be broadened to encompass perceptual and cognitive functions in their entirety. However, it is only in the most recent past that I have begun to reconsider this issue in greater detail, particularly as a consequence of Levin's (1991) work. (For a representation of the revised hierarchical model, see Gedo, 1979a, p. 195.)

I concluded the theoretical section of *Beyond Interpretation* with a chapter on the disarray of psychoanalytic metapsychology. I tried to show that, since the general rejection of Freud's hypothesis of a "death instinct," no alternative had been offered that would have brought the phenomena of the repetition compulsion into the realm of explanation provided by drive theory. Because my latest proposals for a hierarchical model eschewed dealing in satisfactory detail with the problem of motivation, the theoretical system I outlined was still incomplete, and it remained to be seen whether it would eventually gain true coherence through appropriate linkage with consistent, biologically valid propositions about the functioning of the brain.

Shortly after its publication, *Beyond Interpretation* was the subject of a 1981 symposium in the journal *Psychoanalytic Inquiry* (vol. 1, no. 2). A distinguished roster of commentators responded, for the most part, to the theory of psychoanalytic technique contained in the book–a bias I had promoted through my choice of a title that focused attention on that issue. Only Gill (1981) had the discernment–while reserving overall judgment on the theories proposed–to pinpoint the seeming inadequacy of the hypothesis offered to link the biological sources of motivation with subjective intentionality. He called the concept of repetition compulsion a "slender reed" for the purpose of providing such a connection.

In my attempt to answer the objections of my critics (Gedo, 1981a), I responded to Gill's challenge as follows:

> I continue to adhere to the conclusion Freud reached in 1920: that our clinical work fails to unearth subjective wishes to account for a

---

[3] This line of development corresponds to the concept of self used by a number of authors (e.g., Lichtenberg, 1983; Stern, 1985)–one focused on the subjective experience of one's own person.

variety of maladaptive behaviors. I have added the hypothesis that the realm of subjectivity also fails to account for other behaviors, both useful and pleasurable, which are compulsively repetitive. Such phenomena have tended not to elicit psychoanalytic scrutiny because they are not pathological. Gill is correct in discerning that this idea is the biological bedrock of my overall proposal [pp. 300–301].

Further, I asserted that my hypotheses lay within the boundaries of natural science because I conceived of the self-organization "as the sum of those psychobiological patterns that become obligatory components of the compulsion to repeat" (p. 309). One prominent class of patterns of this kind is the need actively to repeat archaic affective states. Another way to put these points is that a theory of self-organization consists of an inclusive hierarchy of personal aims. Hence the task of the hierarchical model is to portray "the manner in which the regulation of behavior at prepsychological (i.e., presymbolic), psychological (symbolic), and transitional levels [may] be conceptualized in one inclusive and consistent theory" (p. 312).

The concept of repetition compulsion "explains that early biological experiences which, from our usual psychological perspective, are passively endured, affect later behavior through automatic repetition in the active mode – hence, as Freud continued to insist, the unconscious is ultimately unknowable because whatever we need to repeat has no mental (i.e., symbolic) representation" (pp. 314–315). I concluded by noting that we need to understand better how "stable patterns of stimulation and affective response [are maintained] through active mechanisms seeking to restore previous equilibria" (p. 315) – a question to which answers have to be provided by research into the functions of the brain.

It may be relevant to repeat at this point that the pertinent neurophysiological data were recently summarized by Hadley (1989). In her view, these findings are generally congruent with the contentions of Lichtenberg (1989), who postulated five distinct preprogrammed biological patterns of motivation. Lichtenberg called these motivational systems attachment, sensuality/sexuality, aversion, active exploration, and the maintenance of physiological equilibria. It remains to be seen whether this list is complete and definitive.

As I see this issue, such blueprints for behavior operate in pure culture only during phase I (i.e., in mode I). Depending on the affective coloring they acquire at that time, the individual will seek to repeat a hierarchy of *experiential* patterns. This is why the various prepro-grammed motivational alternatives play such different roles in the psychic lives of different individuals. At the same time, behavior in subsequent modes continues to be classifiable only according to a schema of biologically programmed motivations – one cannot live life divorced from a body. But these basic blueprints are assimilated through the mediation of affectivity into a need to repeat a set of concrete experiential states. As George Klein (1976, pp. 114–115) put this, the memories of previous sensual experiences are organized into cognitive schemata. (For a more detailed examination of these princi-ples and their applicability to a view of sexuality within the hierar-chical schema, see Gedo, 1979a, pp. 183–184.)

FURTHER CLINICAL APPLICATIONS

Through the 1980s, I tried to document the clinical usefulness of the hierarchical model in a series of reports focused on specific topics. Perhaps the most significant of these was an effort to apply this conceptual tool to the problem of "choice of symptom" (Gedo, 1981b, chap. 12). By means of a case illustration showing that, as a result of developmental progress, addictive behaviors may spontaneously turn into fetishistic perversion (and in stressful circumstances this evolution may be reversed), I tried to highlight that the choice between these alternative symptom clusters was determined by the specific mode of functioning to which the analysand regressed (from a tenuous adapta-tion generally maintained in mode IV whenever human assistance was steadily available).

Yet the identification of the symptom's adaptive function is not sufficient by itself to explain the specific configuration the symptom comes to assume. In order to understand the manner in which this configuration is reached, other developmental issues must be consid-ered – those of the particular meanings attributable to the behavior in question in the historical context wherein it arose, that is, in a specific developmental phase. Thus, an addiction may be extremely archaic from a functional viewpoint; yet, if it arises relatively late in the course of development, it may represent a neurotic compromise forma-tion by means of regressive mechanisms. When, in the case reported, maturation rendered the pacifying function of the addictive behavior superfluous, it acquired a variety of symbolic meanings once again referable to the historical context of this altered situation – mostly meanings that could buttress self-esteem through fantasies of perfection in the phallic sphere and, at the same time, avoid guilt-provoking clashes with essential objects. These intersecting vectors leading to particular symptomatic behaviors are best understood in terms of the availability of a range of functional modes in the relevant phases of development.

Another distinction that is greatly facilitated by the hierarchical model is that between an arrest of development and functional regression from developmentally more advanced positions, a matter also taken up in *Advances in Clinical Psychoanalysis* (Gedo, 1981b, chap. 13). As for the etiology of arrestation, I suggested (on the basis of clinical material) that development could not proceed whenever a child confronts the challenges of the present with psychological dispositions that reflect unsuccessful solutions for those of previous developmental phases. In particular, the demands of the oedipal period (phase IV) are usually insurmountable if the child, upon entry into this new arena, is still struggling with unfinished problems from its past – in other words, if its current behavior is for the most part organized in the more archaic modes (see also Gedo, 1981b, chap. 14). Another way to put this is that "most of the ego defenses which serve to ward off oedipal strivings consist of behaviors that constitute, at the same time, adaptive solutions to the psychological vicissitudes of still earlier phases of development" (Gedo, 1984, p. 6).

A few years later, I attempted to reassess the place of the hierarchical view of mental life within the evolution of psychoanalytic ideas (Gedo, 1984, chap. 1) by putting forward the claim that it constitutes an insistence on the import of the structural (i.e., biological) viewpoint, in contrast to the emphasis on mental contents that had characterized psychoanalysis for several decades. In particular, the

> hierarchical model stresses the fact that psychological maturation involves the acquisition of competence with respect to a progressively expanding list of specific mental and behavioral skills . . . . Competence in the domain of certain crucial mental capacities enables an individual to confront the challenges of subsequent developmental phases. If . . . an individual is deficient with respect to certain requisite skills, this deficiency . . . may have to be patched over

through external assistance. The need to find symbiotic partners who can render such aid leads to the manifold behavioral potentialities . . . labeled "archaic transferences" in the analytic setting [p. 8].[4]

At this time, I catalogued the adaptive solutions available in the various modes of structuralization as follows:

[In] mode I [there is only] resort to the biological resources of the organism; from a strictly "psychological" viewpoint . . . experience in this mode is endured passively. The child has acquired the capacities [of] mode II when, as a matter of routine, he or she can actively recreate a subset of subjective experiences. Similarly, mode III is attained when the child's characteristic response has changed from the automatic repetition of specific experiences to a holistic program of action . . . . Mode IV, in turn, signifies that the individual need no longer process typical experiences through concrete enactments; instead [they] can [be] mediate[d] . . . through the channel of fantasies . . . . Finally, in mode V, people characteristically make use of their nuclear fantasies in a creative manner as blueprints for constructive activities [p. 15].

It should be noted that the transitions between modes are attributed to new cognitive achievements that have not at this point been incorporated into the model's 1979 version.

It was Lichtenberg (1983) who first published specific examples of various regulatory or cognitive deficits that proved to be severe enough to interfere with expectable structuralization of the self. In a commentary on his work, I (Gedo, 1986, chap. 12) noted once again that a child impaired in this manner must inevitably rely on external assistance to adapt to the escalating demands of life. Hence, a persisting need for symbiosis is the general end result of such a condition. A symbiotic adaptation is often accompanied by illusions of grandiosity to compensate for the attendant humiliations. My essential agreement with Lichtenberg's clinical observations therefore also compelled me to reconsider the developmental line of the cognitive functions in the hierarchical model, which were not sufficiently elaborated to deal with the kind of data he chose to highlight. As an example of the kind of

---

[4] To illustrate the utility of the hierarchical model in delineating varied states of structuralization, I made use at this time of the illustrative case of differing phenomenology of a "masochistic" and "depressive" nature as correlated with functioning in the various modes, I through V (see Gedo, 1984, p. 14).

concepts needed to illuminate this domain, one might cite the manner in which certain bodily processes of toddlers in the sensorimotor phase might be linked to the emergent capacities to symbolize–usually in terms of verbal codes–or fail to gain this potential for cortical regulation. There are, of course, many other types of cognitive deficit to be considered. (For a clinical example of one of these, see Gedo, 1986, pp. 182–184.) Robbins (1987) soon joined in calling for careful attention to this aspect of development.[5]

THE CURRENT POSITION

Over the years, I gradually realized that one obstacle to ease of utilization of the hierarchical model is that it portrays only expectable developments, whereas clinicians must continually deal with maladaptive derailments of those processes. To mitigate this problem, I decided to outline a psychoanalytic nosology based entirely on the hierarchical view of mental life, a project that culminated in *The Mind in Disorder* (Gedo, 1988). To accommodate the complexities of perceptual/ cognitive development in the schema, I there proposed a conception of processes taking place on parallel planes, one devoted to the sphere of conflicts, the other to the "quasi-stationary functions" (Rapaport, 1951) that usually develop in a conflict-free manner. Whenever a specific function changes from one of these conditions to the other, this alteration can be noted by means of arrows between the two planes. (For a diagram of these relationships, see Figure 1.) Functions that fail to mature give rise to deficiencies in skills that I termed "apraxias." (In a discussion of this idea, Robbins [1988] made the fine suggestion that, in contrast, the patterning of maladaptive behaviors might be called "dyspraxias." These are manifestations of the need to repeat established properties of the personality.)[6] Until the 1988 modification, the hierarchical model was equipped to show only three specific types of

---

[5] Previously, Robbins (1983) had endorsed the hierarchical conception of ordering psychoanalytic data. Because much of his clinical experience was with personalities arrested in (or regressed to) primitive modes, including some schizophrenics, Robbins feels that the more archaic end of the developmental scale needs to be refined into a greater number of subsidiary categories. Grand and his collaborators (1988) have proposed a modification along these lines.

[6] For a thorough discussion of the role of such repetitions in development, see also Malatesta and Wilson (1988).

apraxia: problems in tension regulation ("typical" for mode I), difficulties in organizing a coherent program of action ("typical" for mode II), and the inability to renounce illusions (referable to mode III). The latest version of the model has the scope to accommodate an infinite variety of these deficiencies: disorders of thought, communication, learning, planning, affectivity, encoding of bodily signals, etc. (see Gedo, 1988, chaps. 13 and 14).

The developmental theory I espouse involves a combination of cognitive maturation and learning as a result of appropriate nurture. Thus, psychological deficits (apraxias) are merely consequences of the failure to learn. Other maladaptive behaviors consist in the automatized repetition of behavioral patterns learned earlier in life, patterns that have proved to be inappropriate in novel circumstances and are therefore dyspraxic. Progression and regression around nodal points that delimit significant phases are implicit in the very concept of development; the epigenetic model universally accepted within psychoanalysis involves, in addition, the idea of a gradually expanding repertory of modes of organization, all of which remain forever available whenever they might once again prove to be advantageous. This aspect of the conceptual schema makes use of general biological principles, without adding any specifically psychoanalytic propositions. Psychological constructs have to be invoked only for that particular portion of the theory that deals with the processing of symbolic thought.

The foregoing consideration brings us back to the realms of neuroscience. As I noted in chapter 1, it is the development of neural structures that leads to behavioral regulation by means of symbolization, and it is the acquisition of language that seems to lead to a new mode of neural organization. Hence, the most pressing question about the hierarchical model concerns the manner in which it should incorporate the role of language acquisition in personality development. This is the most promising avenue of inquiry into the ways in which biology and the world of the psyche overlap.

CHAPTER 4

• —————————————————— •

Challenge, Apraxia, and Avoidance

A man in his late 30s, who was in the eighth year of an analysis undertaken because of paralyzing difficulties that had driven him to despair, managed, at long last, to fall in love for the first time. Contrary to his invariable habit in relation to the countless women he had discarded in a career of Don Juanism, with his *inamorata* he was not preoccupied with listing her alleged shortcomings of status or prestige. In fact, he was almost craven in his tolerance of her initial lack of commitment to their relationship, and he refrained entirely from objecting to her behavior and preferences, although he often found these difficult to bear. Only certain dreams of vengeance on a woman (in the manifest content sometimes this was explicitly his mother) – especially revenge by means of sexual infidelities – betrayed his rage at these deprivations and that he was once again on the verge of lapsing into the guerrilla warfare that had characterized his dealings with his parents for over three decades.

Given these circumstances, I predicted a rupture of this important relationship – the first contingency to relieve the patient's chronic depressive mood – unless he could make his needs clear to his beloved and gain her cooperation in mitigating his dissatisfactions. Although he was in complete agreement with this pessimistic forecast, the patient could not mobilize himself to discuss these matters with the frustrator. Instead of taking such action, he spent a number of analytic sessions in obsessive rehearsals of how she would fend off or rebut whatever he might call to her attention. This behavior was an exact repetition of his response, relatively early in the analysis, to the need to confront his father about certain financial arrangements between them that no longer suited the patient. He had avoided that confrontation for a long time, ostensibly because of fear of his father's expectable hostile reactions. When, after long delays, he broached the matter in a series of letters, the issue was resolved amicably, and the patient's projective distortions about his father's attitudes toward him were gradually corrected.

On the basis of this precedent, I became aware that the patient's willingness to sacrifice his first loving relationship to a woman amounted to a phobic avoidance of a potential negotiation between them. I pointed out that he had no right to put hostile arguments into the woman's mouth; moreover, as the transaction with his father had shown us, it was quite probable that the only hostility at play was his own. Although he continued to postpone action in the hope of finding some magical solution, the patient did acknowledge that his lover was evidently unaware of his objections to some of her behavior and was likely to be devastated if he abandoned her, as he was now tempted to do.

Not at all coincidentally, it was on Valentine's day that he finally overcame his reluctance to clear the air between them. He opened his session the next morning with a highly distressed account of how incompetent he had been in bringing these matters to her attention. He barely acknowledged in passing that she had been quite accommodating in her response and had only objected to his failure to state his requirements promptly and candidly. Although the interpersonal problem had evaporated, he now felt much worse about the humiliation of having shown himself to be unable to communicate adequately about relatively simple human transactions. What was worse, his lover had revealed that her own failure to discuss their evolving relationship was caused by her dislike of his manner of discourse. Although, needless to say, she did not use technical terms, she accurately pinpointed his obsessional vagueness, his inability to deal with emotions, and his tendency to miss the point when she was not talking in ways intended to be taken literally. The fact that their colloquium had promoted the relationship and prevented a needless rupture did not console the patient for this humiliating revelation of his limitations.

The man whose phobic behavior I have just described had the Pride of Lucifer—or, if you will, he was a Monster of Vanity! When he started his analysis, he had naively self-revealing dreams of walking in ceremonial processions while clad in a cape the size of a football field...Of course, it was the priority he always gave to status and prestige (to be more accurate, the priority these had acquired when his initial love for his mother had curdled under the impact of her cruel disregard for his needs) that led to his disastrous policy of avoiding potential humiliation. Yet we would be unjustified if we disregarded his claim that the avoidance of confrontation also served to forestall certain anxieties—castration fear in relation to his father and fear of the loss of love of his woman friend—for he was just as limited in his capacity to deal with an upsurge of affect as he was handicapped in discussions of emotional transactions. In other words, any outbreak of anxiety was likely to humiliate him as well.

The probable connection of phobic avoidances with an inability to deal with mounting affect (anxiety) was also noted by Kohut (1984, pp. 28–32) in the specific instance of agoraphobia: he postulated that this syndrome, which is generally mitigated in the presence of a familiar person, betokens an inability to soothe oneself. This suggested explanation properly differentiates between the cause of the anxiety in question (let us say, as traditional interpretations would have it, the sexual temptations of the agora) and that of the final symptom, the phobic avoidance. In his brief excursus on this subject, Kohut failed to consider why many people find it intolerable to *experience* unrelieved anxiety, even if this choice leads to severe self-restrictions. Nor did he address himself to the question whether analogous disabilities in self-regulation may lie behind phobias unrelieved by the availability of human assistance.

As the clinical illustration with which this chapter begins suggests, one possible link between deficits in self-regulation and a policy of avoidance (i.e., the establishment of a phobia) is an inability to accommodate to circumstances understood as humiliations. In my clinical experience with the psychoanalytic method, I have encountered no other linkages of this kind, although this does not mean, of course, that they do not exist. At any rate, for the time being we can postulate that, in childhood, if such intolerance for humiliation does not stand in the way, deficits in autoregulatory capacities will be overcome through the educational efforts of the caretakers. The response of my patient's lover to his mastery of the phobic behavior constitutes the first step in his *Nacherziehung* (to use Freud's term): she instructed him in the precise nature of the psychological skills he needed to acquire. As I have stated elsewhere (Gedo, 1988, Epilogue), one way to conceptualize psycho-analysis-as-treatment is to regard it as a technology of such remedial education in a series of missing skills (the "ego deficits" I prefer to call "apraxias").

In psychoanalytic practice, I have observed a wide variety of avoidant behaviors caused by the foregoing dynamic constellation. For instance, one man entirely avoided social relations with women for several decades because he was afraid that if he attempted sexual relations he might fail in a humiliating manner because of a need to inhibit certain perverse inclinations. Neither was he able to channel his sexual excitement by interposing a layer of fantasy between his inter-personal transactions and his subjective experience, nor could he nego-tiate mutual accommodation with a potential sexual partner. Be it noted that the avoidance of women did not supervene until well past adolescence, a period when this person unselfconsciously acted out his perverse impulses. His horizons subsequently expanded, and his stan-dards of behavior were markedly raised by his gradual absorption of upper middle-class values; his behavior became phobic only when he lost his shamelessness.

At the opposite extreme we find cases of the infernal pride I noted in the young man who dreamed of being the star of princely ceremo-nials. One such person, who was the favored child of a schizophrenic mother with megalomanic ideas, led a life of schizoid withdrawal in order to avoid ordinary human experiences, for these had humiliating connotations for him. Like Shakespeare's Bottom, he expected himself to be vastly superior to mere mortals, as his mother had indicated he was. When explanations of this kind challenged this man to attempt to overcome his avoidance of social relations, he was initially so clumsy that he did, in fact, embarrass himself on various occasions. It was noteworthy that these trivial *faux pas* enraged him with me, because he held me responsible for exposing him to potentially humiliating situa-tions. In other words, he was of the character type excessively vulner-able in terms of self-esteem that Kohut (1971) singled out as the "narcissistic personality disorder."

So-called counterphobic behaviors may be understood to be caused by very similar preferences to preserve false pride at the expense of adaptation; they might be termed instances of "there is nothing to be ashamed of but fear itself." Viewed in this way, these patterns of action actually constitute veritable phobias, and the term "counterphobic" is a misnomer for them. In other words, the mastery of a counterphobic pattern is contingent on a lowering of false pride and does not risk the emergence of an *avoidance* of the action that was previously engaged in compulsively. For example, one patient who rushed in where angels fear to tread in attempting to keep crazy women happy was enacting a grandiose fantasy he needed for complex reasons referable to his situation in early childhood. When we succeeded in clarifying these issues in the analysis, he divorced his psychotic spouse, but this sensible course of action did not render him fearful about holding his own with her or with other crazy people. It makes good sense to understand the clinical gain in this case as the mastery of a phobic avoidance of the shameful status of a "quitter."

All the cases I have cited thus far conform to the hypothesis put forward by Moraitis (1991) to the effect that what the phobic person is actually avoiding is a situation of novelty. Because Moraitis is mainly concerned with a theory of knowledge, his hypothesis is focused on mental contents, and in those terms it seems to be entirely correct. For my patient the Prince, it was the effort to understand the subjectivity of a beloved person that was unprecedented; for the person with perverse sexuality, it would have been the requirement to put the needs of another ahead of his own wishes; for the schizoid patient, it was social relations of a conventional kind; for the "counterphobic" man, it was the acknowledgment that he was vulnerable to the disruptions caused by his crazy wife. The common denominator in every instance was the inability of each person to deal successfully with the new challenge in an age-appropriate manner. Moraitis has a valid insight that can best be turned to account if we realize that novelty represents an adaptive challenge that calls for the deployment of manifold psychological capacities.

I am well aware that the illustrative material I have presented consists entirely of cases wherein the situation feared and avoided was directly discernible, in contrast to the conventional examples of phobia that are complicated by displacement of the fear onto a symbol. The classic case is that of the zoophobia of Little Hans (Freud, 1909a) – a boy in an oedipal crisis whose ambivalence toward his father and fears of retaliation were condensed in the fear of being attacked by a horse and a consequent avoidance of going into the street. I have chosen illustrative cases without this superimposition of defensive distortions precisely to facilitate understanding by focusing on the simplest of instances.

I believe, however, that a childhood zoophobia also needs to be understood in terms of a fear of self-regulatory failure – although, in the oedipal period, the inability to contain anxiety without resort to defensive operations (the apraxia Freud, 1926, called the "actual neurotic core" of a neurosis, that is, the propensity to be overwhelmed by affect) is still more or less age appropriate. Nonetheless, I assume that if this deficit is severe enough to lead to the formation of a childhood neurosis in the form of a phobia, as it did in the case of Little Hans, the child must be attempting to avoid the repeated humiliation of experiencing mounting anxiety without the resources to cope with it.

It is useful to recall in this connection that childhood zoophobias tend to be self-limiting; in latency, they are generally folded into a character neurosis, often of an obsessional type. Such a solution is contingent on a regression to more primitive fantasy systems – in the case of obsessional personalities, to fantasies of an anal-sadistic variety. Another way to view this substitution of a deformation of character for a preexisting phobia is to recall the common finding that in the course of analyzing neurotic characters, the advent of a full-blown transference neurosis may be heralded by the emergence of the affect connected to a long-forgotten zoophobia. These commonplaces of developmental psychology may be more understandable if we keep in mind that the choice of the phobic symptom is dictated by the child's immaturity in mastering anxiety. (This is why we can assure analysands that as adults they should be able to "work through" a transference neurosis involving the very same conflicts that defeated them as children.) The return of derivatives of the childhood symptom in the course of analysis betokens the voluntary relaxation of the defenses originally used to fend it off; what we call the process of working through, then, consists of the gradual acquisition of self-regulatory capacities in the face of anxiety. Moreover, in most cases the reemergence of the childhood fear does not compel the adult analysand to engage in *avoidances*; it is much more usual to experience the repetition in the form of anxiety dreams. We help the working-through process by teaching analysands that their own emotions will not hurt them. Of course, this is done not by making pronouncements to that effect but by arranging for the analysand to experience that he or she can live through these affective storms, simply by tolerating them as they naturally occur in the course of the analysis.

If the avoidance of the symbol for a situation of danger does not differ in principle from a direct avoidance of such a threat, what, then, constitutes the essential distinction between Little Hans and the various Little Princes I have described here? The most direct answer to this question involves the point implicit in the pun I have just used: Little Hans apparently saw himself as an ordinary little boy full of silly ideas; my analysands, in contrast, were full of grandiose notions of their extraordinary worth and superhuman capacities. Whereas Hans was struggling with the putative dangers of retaliation for his oedipal hostilities, Little Princes are only threatened by a potential disillusionment concerning their status and prestige. *Pari passu*, the defenses typically brought into play in these distinctive circumstances are also different; as Freud's follow-up almost two decades after the child's treatment revealed, Little Hans resolved the affair by obliterating his memory of it – repression proper supervened. In each of the cases I have cited in this chapter, it was disavowal that carried the primary burden of defense. Relevant memories from childhood were freely available for recall, but their significance was not acknowledged.

In terms of the hierarchical model of psychic functioning, the conditions characteristic of the childhood neurosis of Little Hans are collectively designated as Mode IV, which is age appropriate for an oedipal child. The capacity to make use of symbolization and displacement as additional defensive operations is an equally expectable part of the cognitive armamentarium at these age levels. By contrast, the mental dispositions I have attributed to the analysands I describe here characterize Mode III in the hierarchical schema. That these individuals failed to make use of the age-appropriate symbolic capacities that eventually became available to them in order to disguise the real issues they needed to avoid betrays the relatively archaic origin of their difficulties; their defensive posture has become structured prior to the secure acquisition of these cognitive skills.

The ability to master the "actual neurotic core" produced by a severe intrapsychic conflict marks the passage from Mode IV to Mode V, that of expectable adult functioning. In other words, when a person learns to regulate his own affective reactions without external assistance and without resort to defensive distortions, there is no further need for symptom formation. At the other end of the developmental scale, do we encounter phobias even more archaic in structure than those I have placed in the category of Mode III? Although persons whose usual level of functioning is in Mode II are unable to cope outside of a sheltered environment, we do occasionally treat analytic patients who generally function on a higher level but demonstrate the continuing influence of a split-off nucleus of mentation organized in a maximally primitive manner. To facilitate the consideration of this topic, I shall briefly present some data from such a case. (I have previously discussed other aspects of this analysis in Gedo, 1981b, chap. 7, case 15.)

This analysand also lived the life of a Prince–roughly in the manner of the Student Prince of operetta fame–but he was haunted by a disabling obsessional symptom, a preoccupation with the possibility that he might not be able to continue breathing. If he did not have a therapist available, in a manner analogous to an iron lung, this anxiety about the absence of self-regulation (made concrete in a single physiological function) verged on panic. Consequently, he had been in more or less continuous therapy since late adolescence. This state of affairs was established when the nursemaid who had raised him since early childhood retired; a few years earlier, when she had first thought of leaving, there was a briefer premonitory outbreak of the same hypochondriacal syndrome.

During the regime of the reliable nursemaid, the only obvious sign of serious psychopathology was a water phobia, which persisted through the patient's latency. To be more precise, the boy avoided occasions when he was expected to go swimming. The anxiety implicit in these situations was that he might drown, or, to put it in a way that connects this symptom with the hypochondriacal one that succeeded it, that he would be prevented from breathing. The symptom was most prominent when the boy was sent away to summer camp, that is, when his nursemaid would not be available. It was not entirely clear just when the phobia started, but it does not seem likely that opportunities to go swimming presented themselves much before latency.

On the basis of the analytic work, we arrived at the conclusion that the fear of drowning was, for this man, an echo of earlier fears of succumbing to the pull for symbiotic fusion with an enormously seductive, intrusive, egocentric, and infantile mother. During the oedipal period, the boy had been made to feel that he was the most important person in her orbit. This privileged position entailed the responsibility of meeting her infinite emotional demands – a situation in which he certainly felt out of his depth. It was against the seductive pull of this dangerous liaison that the prosaic but commonsensical nursemaid provided an effective counterweight. When the boy was allowed to live out the grandiose fantasy of being his mother's lover, his inability to satisfy her sufficiently to keep her from getting depressed perpetually threatened traumatically to deflate him. (These issues were relived in the analytic transference with the roles reversed – he played the part of his childhood mother, and he tried to make me feel helpless and inadequate, as he had been made to feel when he was invited into her bed.)

The water phobia constituted a childhood neurosis wherein the symptom made use of a minimal displacement by way of the concretization of the subjective fantasy of being helpless, unsupported, and overwhelmed. In this sense, water did not constitute an abstract symbol of the engulfing mother; rather, the putative sensation of drowning was a concrete analogue for the quality of the mother–child relationship. I make the assumption that this equivalence was established in the oedipal period on the basis of prior transactions that did not permit this child to maintain his independent volition vis-à-vis his tyrannical mother. It should be noted that the maternal grandmother was on the scene for the first two years of the patient's life and apparently served as an alternative to the mother, as the nursemaid (hired when the grandmother unexpectedly died) was to do afterward. Thus, from the dawn of consciousness, this child had two sets of experiences that could not be integrated with each other – neither could be labeled "true" or "false," à la Winnicott (1954), but there remained a cleavage between them in the manner familiar to us from cases in which those labels apply.

If my reconstruction in this case is valid (a hypothesis supported but not substantiated by the excellent therapeutic outcome), it follows that the phobia, established because of the unmanageable anxieties stirred up by the Pyrrhic victory of the oedipal child, was operative in a segment of mental life seemingly structured in a manner expectable in Mode IV. However, this arrangement of psychic dispositions could only be maintained with external support; when such assistance was unavailable, a much more primitive aspect of functioning became manifest, that of a severe hypochondriasis. This state corresponds to Mode II in the hierarchical schema, most clearly because of the coexistence of differently structured nuclei of function, one hypochondriacal, the other self-observing. The hypochondriacal preoccupation is a desperate effort to ward off the threat of disintegration into total confusion (see Gedo, 1979a, pp. 210–213). In a certain sense, even its manifest content ("I cannot control my breathing") cries from the rooftops that self-regulation is out of the question. When this state of desperate disrepair is covered over by a relationship that amounts to a covert symbiosis, the phobic symptom serves as a warning signal of the dangers implicit in giving in to the temptations of grandiose enterprises.

Of course, in this case, as in that of my other Princes, improvement was contingent on curbing the presumption of claiming to be able to accomplish the impossible, a grandiosity that also constituted an identification with the mother's megalomania. The patient was, metaphorically, ever in danger of drowning in his mother's craziness, unless a very sober person held him back from jumping into that deep water. In this instance, therefore, the daunting challenge to be met was not that of novelty but of the potentialities inherent in regression to the most archaic modes of functioning within the patient's behavioral repertory. Hence this illustration conforms to the explanation Kohut (1971) offered for the acrophobias: he postulated that those who are afraid of heights are tempted to enact the grandiose fantasy of being able to fly. In this sense, both acrophobia and the water phobia I have described constitute adaptive responses to the potential activation of a "psychotic core" in the depths. The reality ego rightly says, "Get thee behind me, Satan!"

Phobias, like people, are more complex than we like to believe. And there is no way to predict which of the challenges a person may experience he may feel shamefully unprepared to meet.

CHAPTER 5

• ———————————————— •

Obsessionality, Magical Beliefs, and the Hierarchical View of Mental Life

Not long ago, Freedman (in Panel, in prep.) introduced a reconsideration of obsessional phenomena by pointing out that obsessionality is encountered in a broad range of circumstances, from clear-cut instances of neurosis to certain neurophysiological contingencies. As the clinical material discussed on that occasion demonstrated, conditions between these extremes on the continuum of nosological possibilities varied from crises of unmanageable stress in early childhood to the boundaries of psychotic decompensation in adult life. As Freedman stated, the distinction between obsessional neurosis and obsessional phenomena of other kinds had already been made by Freud (1905b) in discussing the case of Dora.

In obsessional neurosis, the symptomatology is causally related to the recurrence of intrapsychic conflicts of oedipal origin, and the choice of symptoms is determined by anxiety-based regression to the emotional world of the anal phase of psychosexual development. As Dowling (in Panel, in prep.) convincingly showed in his presentation of such a case, the obsessions signified the creation of painful and inconvenient anal "messes" and, at the same time, represented regressive compromise formations that permitted the avoidance of anxiety about fantasied castration. On a more fundamental level, however, the symptom constituted part of the abiding fabric of the patient's mental life. As Dowling put this, they amounted to the adaptive use of thinking in order to contain action. Needless to say, from a different vantage point, they may be seen as a miscarriage of the effort to adapt.

As Dowling's analysand improved, by mastering his castration anxiety and rendering superfluous any libidinal regression, his propensity for obsessional thinking did not disappear but seemed to undergo a change of function. In the analyst's words, the obsessional phenomena now became "a companion, a source of consolation, and a friend." Dowling therefore postulated that the obsessionality had its genesis before the formation of the infantile neurosis in the oedipal period. In other words, the regression under the impact of castration anxiety did not constitute a return to a libidinal fixation point alone; it was also a matter of making additional use of an established adaptive device. In the case under discussion, this was initially established very early in childhood, presumably as a buffer against severe blows to the patient's self-esteem, caused by disappointments inflicted by the primary caretakers. In the vocabulary of Winnicott (1951), the obsessions had their genesis as "transitional phenomena."

From a developmental perspective, it seems that a specifically obsessional manner of processing thoughts need not constitute a regressive phenomenon at all. Nor does it invariably entail a return to anal preoccupations in terms of mental contents, as the traditional formulation of obsessional neurosis would predict. Rather, obsessionality may always remain an essential component of a given person's adaptive repertory–a tool for the regulation of tension levels, to ward off isolation and a sense of emptiness, to signal the need for caution or vigilance. Adaptive needs of this kind are potentially present from the cradle to the grave. Obsessionality amounts to the crystallization of a cognitive style at the very dawn of symbolic thinking.

In this regard, it is necessary to keep in mind the distinction between obsessionality and magical thinking, phenomena frequently associated with each other, a point also emphasized by Freedman (in Panel, in prep.). Areas of magical thinking may persist into adulthood in people whose predominant behavior is in most other respects impeccably rational. Conditions of this kind are brought about as a consequence of profound cleavages in the personality, developed very early in life. As a result of such failures of integration or of defensive splitting, arrests of development may involve only those segments of the personality that constitute one side (or another) of such a divided personality. Hence, in principle, anyone may have either an obsessional nucleus or one of magical thinking within the overall organization of mental life, and such a "nucleus of the self" (Gedo and Goldberg, 1973) may be used more or less frequently throughout the life course as an adaptive resort in emergency situations.

Chused (in Panel, in prep.) has described several children in analysis who used magical rituals in conditions of acute stress as temporary measures to preserve equilibrium. In other words, not only does obsessionality exist outside the boundaries of "neurosis," but so do compulsive activities as well. (Chused astutely points out that analysts may use their therapeutic procedures as magical rituals of this kind whenever they feel helpless!) The other side of this coin is that neither obsessional thinking nor the ritual use of magic is normally to be found in young children. Assertions that children believe in the omnipotence of thoughts (first made in the psychoanalytic literature in 1913 by Ferenczi) confuse magical beliefs with the ignorance of causality that is characteristic of the very young. The naive youngster's limited understanding of the actualities of this world may be ameliorated through the instruction provided by trusted caretakers. By contrast, magical beliefs cannot be corrected by means of remedial instruction.

Magical thinking is, in other words, a fixed cognitive schema. Patients may or may not give full credence to their magical schemata, for the irrational beliefs may in fact come to be disavowed, in preference to their renunciation and the potential anxiety that may follow. It was Rapaport (1951) who first called to the attention of psychoanalysts the fact that magical belief systems are not the direct consequences of primary process thinking—in other words, that these belief systems are probably *learned*. Hence it is no oversimplification to conceive of the persistence of disavowed magical beliefs as the conflict between clashing *Weltanschauungen*, those of rationalism and those of a crude private religion. Freud (1913) was, of course, first to point to the poorly defined boundary area between totemism (as a form of religion) and obsessions. Yet we may be mistaken in looking upon patients' magical beliefs as "private." They may appear to be so only because we are ignorant of the influence of our patients' coreligionists, the caretakers whose faith they have adopted.

In this regard, a case I published some years ago (Gedo, 1979a, chaps. 8 and 9) provides a cogent example: This patient's seemingly self-destructive, magical reliance on the effects of his moral rectitude on the force of destiny, without his taking the actions necessary to safeguard his best interests, turned out to be the consequence of an identification with his beloved primary caretaker, an admired grandmother from whom he had been separated at the age of about five. This woman had a private religion, largely based on certain well-known Far Eastern prototypes, that was impregnated with magical beliefs about the power of spiritual "goodness." My analysand was entirely unaware that his behavior continued to be guided by his grandmother's precepts, although he was quite capable of describing them accurately and did not consciously agree with them. Nor did his eventual realization that these old beliefs were still decisive in determining his actions suffice to terminate their influence without a considerable internal struggle. Confronted by the consequences of relying on magic, a normal two-year-old would simply accept the parents' word that God helps only those who help themselves.

In the foregoing instance, the acceptance of a magical belief system could not be regarded as maladaptive in the context of the analysand's childhood, but it proved to be terribly inconvenient in adult life. Despite his magical beliefs, this patient was not obsessional, still less did he suffer from obsessional neurosis. His unusual personality was formed on the basis of conflicting identifications. These sources of unintegrated behavior proved to be relatively easy to reconcile, and an unusually felicitous analytic result was obtained after a mere 15 months of treatment. I stress that the magical beliefs did not form part of an obsessional syndrome, in order to underscore the conclusion that these groups of phenomena – magic versus obsessions – are distinct and by no means invariably linked. I have had clinical experience in analysis with a number of patients who engaged in magical thinking without being obsessional – for example, a gambler spurred on by magical expectations, or a sufferer from a masochistic perversion who continued to believe in superstitions learned from a bizarre mother.

I have also analyzed a number of patients of obsessional *character* who did not manifest any evidence of magical thinking. Chused (in Panel, in prep.) reports on the analysis of a latency-age boy whose treatment was successful but eventuated in the formation of such an obsessional personality. In addition to the weight of such analytic evidence, we commonly encounter people paralyzed by pervasive doubts and ambivalence, those who suffer from isolation of affect or alexithymia and those who tend to intellectualization as well as to the pattern called "doing and undoing." These obsessional phenomena may be found as a cluster or as isolated symptoms, with or without magical thinking. Moreover, they may or may not be accompanied by a regression to the realm of anality. Broad clinical experience does not confirm the claim of Anna Freud (1966), that obsessionality comes about if the ego matures too early, so that expectable anal-sadistic traits are prematurely experienced as intolerable and have to be countered by means of "primitive" mechanisms of defense available at the time—isolation of affect, doing and undoing, and so on.

In the clearest relevant instance I have dealt with (reported at greater length in Gedo, 1988, chap. 14), the genesis of an obsessional syndrome (characterized by intellectualization as well as doing and undoing) took place in the second year of life, in the context of the disruption of the child's relationship to his mother during the preverbal era. Here it may be sufficient to mention that the mother had her next baby when the analysand was a year old, and she was far along in her third pregnancy before he reached the age of two. Transference developments—not to speak of the entire life history!—testified to the fact that the future patient responded to these childhood stresses with grief, humiliation, and rage. (Chused [in Panel, in prep.] found the very same affective responses underlying the obsessionality of children in analysis with her.) I should stress, however, that for my patient the most damaging aspect of the childhood situation was his loss of trust in human assistance, a matter also relevant in relation to the clinical material cited by Dowling and Chused at the recent Panel.

Such alienation deprives children of the kind of essential parental input, communication in language that may eventually be shared, that may permit symbolic encoding of the affective reactions in question. In the case I just summarized, the child never learned to monitor his subjective world in terms of any consensual symbolic code, except perhaps for the development of a pervasive vigilance for the potential of being humiliated—he was almost entirely alexithymic. This cognitive limitation was largely responsible for his propensity to doubt his judgment and to lapse into ambivalence. It also predisposed him to engage in intellectualization: This person was generally trying to plan his behavior, ineffectually, on the basis of external cues alone, without the essential information provided by spontaneous emotional responses to various contingencies. Thus, he could not formulate subjec tive attitudes to whatever he encountered and had to rely on prescriptions learned by rote.

Another way to approach the phenomena encountered in this case is to characterize the patient's principal motivations throughout life in terms of a need to master, through reversal, the traumata imposed on him so early in life: he wished to frustrate and shame his caretakers. In this instance, perhaps we may attribute the absence of anal fixation to the circumstance that these hostile aims could not be accomplished through misbehavior in habit training, for the child's bodily care had been delegated to hired servants. In order to have any impact on the parents, the child's negativism had to be much more pervasive. The only measure striking enough to disturb the child's mother was to arouse her expectations about some course of action and then not to follow through with it: doing and undoing in the service of scorching the earth. As a consequence, this patient literally never learned how to plan goal-directed behavior – he remained focused almost exclusively on whether or not his actions were pleasing or displeasing to others.

I trust the foregoing summary is not too condensed to convey the flavor of an obsessional syndrome that crystallized not because of the premature development of drive controls, as Anna Freud (1966) would have it. On the contrary, it came into being as a consequence of functional deficits and severe traumata. I have tried to highlight two clusters of cognitive functions the development of which is distorted in this syndrome: 1) those subserving recognition and symbolic processing of the world of subjectivity, and 2) those leading to coherent behavior through the exercise of rational planning. I believe it is reasonably clear that, whenever these cognitive functions remain deficient, the bewilderment produced by this deficit would be relieved most easily if the child could in fact attain magical powers! Because this patient never resorted to magical thinking, he remained confused a great deal of the time.

The kind of traumatic genesis of obsessionality I have just tried to outline constitutes one pole on a continuum within which the opposite pole is represented by the circumstances described earlier in this chapter by means of the example of the analysis reported by Dowling (Panel, in prep.). One might say that in that instance the analysand used his own thinking as a transitional experience, having found this autoplastic creative solution for the strains of a difficult early childhood. In contrast, the patient I have just described was the passive victim of an identification with the aggressor that led to alloplastic efforts that progressively cut him off more and more from human assistance.

In the situation created by this isolation from others, even a belief in magic might have produced relief by means of self-soothing. But the style of upbringing within this family did not encourage such fantasies; instead, it taught the child to appreciate his helplessness all too thoroughly. The outcome of the Oedipus complex was consequently also much more unfavorable for my patient than for the one described by Dowling. Instead of being able to form a neurosis (through anal regression and the use of magical rituals), as did Dowling's analysand, the child became even more embittered with both parents as a result of expectable oedipal disappointments. In reaction, he began to have fantasies about humiliating women sexually. As an adult, he was something of a Don Juan, endlessly obsessed with whether it was even worth his while to complete his conquests.

In such a situation, a system of magical beliefs shared by the entire family may serve a child as a life-saving bridge to a sense of community. For example, the gambler I alluded to earlier, who was the neglected runt of a litter of nine children, managed for much of his childhood to maintain a (tenuous) feeling of belonging to his family by absorbing his parents' primitive beliefs in the supernatural. The earliest manifestation of his commitment to magic recorded in the analysis was a memory from the middle of his third year of life, when one of his older brothers was rushed to a hospital for emergency surgery. My patient had then insisted on going to bed for the night with his shoes on, apparently in the belief that this magical ritual would influence his brother's fate. This memory came to light shortly after one of the patient's other brothers committed suicide and several members of the family, including the analysand, felt guilty about not having prevented this outcome through some unspecified (magical) intervention. Not to share such beliefs still amounted to exile from the family communion!

I believe I have now said enough about a variety of obsessional phenomena to justify my skepticism about the value of gathering these heterogeneous behaviors under one rubric. The concept of obsessionality is a purely phenomenological one and properly belongs in the realm of descriptive psychiatry, but not in a psychoanalytic nosological system. Each obsessional phenomenon has a specific meaning for the person who has produced it, a meaning that may change depending on the context. The clinical theories of psychoanalysis allow for sufficient variability to be essentially useless in any attempt to discern a priori the significance of any bit of behavior in a specific instance.

Nonetheless, certain commonalities about obsessional phenomena do remain valid: the motives behind these behaviors are bewilderingly obscure, both to the subject and to external observers; the obsessional thoughts and compulsive rituals are generally devoid of direct affect, albeit interference with such symptomatology will create intense anxiety; in the cognitive sphere, the obsessional betrays a striking concretization of thought, even in the absence of magic. I wish to illustrate these features by means of still another clinical example.

The analytic material in question came into focus as the patient came to grips with the defensive function of certain fantasies about me that had sharply differentiated me from his working-class parents. He reacted with a dream in which he was wearing tattered underwear; he wanted to change into something better but was prevented from doing so by the presence of an older woman. His associations led to his conflicted loyalty to his mother, a topic we had touched on several times in the recent past. I suggested that, because of this loyalty, he had a need to disavow that his parents' peasant ways were humiliating for him. He agreed with this interpretation, and he was reminded of the painful consequences of his father's own efforts to master shame about these matters, his railings against the clergy, the capitalists, the Jews—and against his Americanized children.

In the next session, which followed a weekend interruption, the patient elaborated on his difficulty in acknowledging his realization that the family pathology was not simply cultural in origin—that his father was ever-hovering at the edge of mental illness, which was distressingly common among his relatives. And the next day he asked me whether he had ever mentioned (of course, he had not!) that when he went away to college, he had been haunted by the obsessive thought that his underwear was dirty and smelly. He now realized that this notion must have been connected with the epithets his father had, in former years, hurled at him, in his native Polish; literally translated, the words had been, "Garbage! stinking child! shitty child!" Of course, anyone who left home was a stinking traitor!

The patient next remembered that, at the age of 11 to 12, he had suffered from a full-blown obsessive-compulsive state. At his father's insistence, he had to be in bed by 8 o'clock. While he listened to the happy sounds of other children playing in the street outside his window, he found himself repeating a series of prayers, and he had a need to do this in a perfect manner. The least deviation from the proper way entailed starting over from the beginning of the series, and the intrusion of any *impure* thought constituted an intolerable transgression that had to be expiated by his getting out of bed to kiss the feet of an effigy of Jesus affixed to the wall. Until the ritual was successfully completed, he found it impossible to go to sleep.

The symptoms simultaneously disavowed the searing shame of having a crazy father and the rageful rebellion against him, and they ultimately concretized these "impure" thoughts as literal shittiness. However, by the time the patient reached college, the function of accepting the misattribution of being a stinker had become incomprehensible. Consciously, he felt no guilt about leaving his parents behind and triumphing over his father by joining the educated classes. Nor did he know that one spur to this ambition was his envy and malice, the remaining stigma of an infantile neurosis established in the oedipal period—that is, well before the outbreak of the obsessive-compulsive crisis at the threshold of adolescence.

If my reconstruction of the manner in which the successive developments in the maturation of this personality is acceptable as a reasonable approximation of historical truth, it follows that various aspects of the patient's obsessionality had their genesis in successive phases of childhood. In other words, the clinical picture as a whole is best understood in terms of a hierarchical view of psychic life, such as the one proposed in my previous work (see chapter 4). In the foregoing clinical vignette, the analysand was in the optimal mode of functioning expectable in adulthood, and his introspective efforts (barely bolstered by my articulation of various issues that had become conscious) led to clearer memories of a past regressive episode characterized by an acute neurotic illness—a regression from mode V to mode IV in the hierarchical schema (Gedo and Goldberg, 1973). Instead of presenting further material from this analysis, it may be easier to illustrate a deeper regression (to mode III, a realm of unchallenged illusions) by reference to the case reported by Dowling (in Panel, in prep.), summarized early in this chapter. When that person dealt with castration anxiety by resorting to obsessional ruminations, this was not merely a neurotic compromise formation (in mode IV), as Dowling made clear; it was also an effort to buttress the patient's shaky self-esteem through an illusion of self-sufficiency.[1]

To adumbrate the possibility of even more archaic origins for obsessionality, clinical material from analyses dealing with individuals more impaired than the ones discussed thus far would have to be presented. I can offer relevant data from the lengthy analysis of a schizoid character,[2] much of whose mental activity consisted of obsessional ruminations, often about financial matters or about how he might have obtained better results in some enterprise by pursuing a different course of action (usually unspecified). It gradually became clear that, in contrast to these lamentations, this well educated man never pursued a coherent plan of action. He would, instead, impulsively follow his whims, only to abandon his initial deeds in reflexive undoing. Although it was also true that this man was provocative and negativistic–characterological attributes that soon became components of a tenacious negative transference–not even the mastery of these traits through years of analytic effort succeeded in altering his pattern of thoughtlessness about future activities.

On one level, this structured heedlessness appeared to constitute an identification with the patient's mother, a person who had lapsed into chronic paranoid schizophrenia several years before she gave birth to him. Despite the severity of her impairment, she was maintained at home throughout the patient's upbringing, in which she took the most active role. Her son was the only person able to get along with her without provoking violent outbursts on her part, largely because of his ability to comply with her demands without demurral, and without reflection. But his attunement to her needs (Stern, 1985) was not simply a result of intimidation: it also constituted a strong and exclusive positive bond. (His schizoid characteristics served in large measure to preserve this exclusivity.) Their relationship was erotized in an anal mode: she assaulted him with enemas; he provoked these passive experiences through obstinate pseudonegativism about moving his

---

[1] The patient I described in the brief vignette illustrating obsessionality without resort to magic also illustrates a persistence of functioning in mode III, particularly so because disavowal of the illusions of his early childhood determined the structure of his subsequent personality: that is, it led to a permanent split in his mental life.

[2] I have already alluded to this analysis in chapter 2.

bowels. His failure to plan ahead was, in part, a transference reenactment of this erotized game, but interpretation of its significance did not
enable the patient to overcome this apraxia (Gedo, 1988).

Ultimately, we were unable to discern whether the deficit in
selecting goals and adhering to some program that could achieve them
was simply the consequence of a primary identification with a chronically disorganized schizophrenic. Although adhering to his mother's
ways was, for this analysand, an important by-product of the dynamic
Modell (1965) named "separation guilt," psychoanalytic methods
cannot elucidate whether the deficit was merely learned or, just as
likely, built upon constitutionally determined neurophysiological
foundations—the kinds of obsessionality produced by biological givens
Freedman (in Panel, in prep.) referred to.[3] In any case, the deficit was
already present in early childhood and prevented the organization of a
hierarchy of personal aims. In the hierarchical schema I have devised,
this means that, in the absence of a symbiotic partner who can
compensate for this apraxia, the individual is partially arrested in mode
II. (How such people can function in adult life is discussed at length in
my 1988 book on psychopathology, *The Mind in Disorder*.) These
handicaps naturally tend to produce severe problems in self-esteem, so
that the personality is likely to take on the flavor of a disturbance of
character. Nonetheless, the basic problem may very well be the consequence of the very same genetic flaws that, in the case of the patient's
mother, led to a schizophrenic illness.

---

[3] Unfamiliar as I am with the research literature of neuroscience, I turned to Fred
Levin, author of the recent book (1991) on brain/mind correlations, for guidance on this
issue. Levin believes that the weight of evidence implicates the basal ganglia in a type
of pathology that prevents the screening out of irrelevant information in the process of
decision making.

CHAPTER 6

· ———————————————— ·

Affective Disorders and the Capacity to Modulate Feeling States

Viewed from a functional perspective, affective disorders constitute an apraxia (Gedo, 1988)–a defect in the crucial psychological ability to modulate ordinary emotional responses to the vicissitudes of everyday life. Such a lack in the repertory of adaptive skills may have its roots in innate predisposition; that is, it may be predominantly determined by constitutional factors or early biological noxae. At the other extreme, it may be almost entirely acquired–let us say because of inappropriate affective attunement with the primary caretaker (see Stern, 1985). In the majority of instances, it is probably a convergence of constitutional and environmental factors that produces the defect. In any case, this apraxia creates a vulnerability such that life circumstances that are within the boundaries of the expectable will trigger biological mechanisms (i.e., affective states of depression or elation) that cannot then be brought to a halt by means of appropriate feedback.

My therapeutic experience with problems of this type confirms the accepted view (see Karasu, 1990) that it is easier to reverse such pathological developments by means of pharmacological measures or the provision of a therapeutic symbiosis within a "holding environment" (as Modell, 1975, conceived of this) than through efforts to deal with the causes of the disintegrative process by providing insight. Often it appears that a seemingly well-adapted premorbid state was maintained as a consequence of a more or less covert symbiosis and that the disruption of such an insecure adaptation by the rupture of the symbiotic relationship is the event that precipitates the acute affective illness. I should like to illustrate the foregoing description of such psychopathology through the following clinical example:

CASE #1

Some time ago, I received a panicky call from a woman in academic life who had heard of me as the husband of a successful scholar. She wanted the name of a family therapist to deal with an emergency: her husband, a physician-administrator, had recently undergone a startling personality change and after 15 years of marriage had left their home. I complied with the caller's request, but she soon called again, even more anxiously than before: her husband was unwilling to see anyone about the marriage; how could she get him to accept personal help? I offered to advise her about this if she wished to consult me, and she gratefully took advantage of the opportunity.

I then met an attractive, if careworn, 40-year-old intellectual who talked in a squeaky, mouselike manner, with great prolixity and tangentiality, and was so anxious that she missed the purport of many of my questions. It was immediately clear that, whatever the status of her husband, she herself needed therapeutic assistance, for she was thoroughly bewildered by her situation. She had met her husband as a freshman in college and had scarcely ever dated anyone else. They were married when he finished medical school and she was a graduate student in the humanities. As she saw it, they had lived a harmonious life. They did not have children, and she had been supported in her scholarly ambitions, as she supposed my wife must have been supported by me. Her husband's occupation was much more remunerative than hers, so that she relied on his earnings. Pursuing endeavors that often necessitated lengthy trips abroad, she became more and more specialized in her esoteric subfield. It was while she was spending the previous summer in Europe that her husband deserted her, although he concealed this until her return. He then announced that he was a changed person and would not disclose where he had taken up his domicile.

The patient was able to grasp that she could not force her husband to seek assistance, but she had some difficulty understanding that psychotherapy might help her to sort out how she had fallen victim to some illusion. The obstacle proved to be her adherence to the medical judgment of her husband, who insisted that all she needed was a tranquilizer to calm her down. In fact, she was taking enough of the medication he had provided for her to cause some friends falsely to conclude that she had become an alcoholic. I was shocked to learn that he was also "treating" her for a recurrence of duodenal ulcer symptoms, in a manner that struck me as much less than adequate. I therefore advised her in the most emphatic terms to consult a reliable internist and gradually to cut back on her use of the tranquilizer; I told her that her husband's management of her health problems amounted to malpractice, if not criminal negligence, and I compared her situation to that of the heroine of the celebrated Ingrid Bergman movie *Gaslight* (see Calef and Weinshel, 1981).

In response to these forceful interventions, the patient confessed that her mother had been telling her the very same things, but she could not bear to accept this version of reality. Because she had so much respect for my wife, with some of whose writings she was familiar, she would provisionally take my word for what constituted reality and would accept treatment, although she could not guarantee that her husband would even be willing to sign medical insurance forms on her behalf. He was continuing to pay her bills, provided she asked no questions and did as she was told. I agreed to take responsibility for her care if she would consult an attorney about her legal rights.

For the next eight weeks, before I went on a month's vacation, we met somewhat irregularly, no more than 20 times, to clarify the situation further and formulate a treatment plan. Meanwhile, she established that her husband was living with another woman; a number of her acquaintances had been aware of his infidelities for some time. She tried to disavow the significance of his duplicitous behavior through pseudofeminist slogans that all men are like that, but she had to face the fact that she did not think *I* was that kind of person. She had sought me out because she felt certain that the woman whose works she so admired could not be married to a scoundrel. And she realized that it was her thrice-divorced mother whose delusional ideas about men she had been parroting.

The patient was the only child of her parents, although her father had children from his two previous marriages. The parents were divorced when the patient was three, and thereafter the mother tried to turn the child against her father, who died about two years later. Subsequently, contact with her paternal family, including her half-siblings, was completely interdicted, and the patient felt trapped in a suffocating relationship with her mother, whose remarriage and third divorce only added to the daughter's disgust and disillusionment. It was with a sense of liberation that she accepted a scholarship to a prestigious college far from her mother's home, and she immersed herself in her studies with great enthusiasm. It was in this context that she formed her alliance with her husband-to-be, and she now realized that he had served as a substitute for the intrusive and controlling mother. Nonetheless, when my scheduled vacation supervened, she was still focused on saving her marriage, although she was considerably calmer and had much less false optimism about the prospect of managing this.

I arranged to refer the patient to a competent colleague, but she made it clear that she was unwilling to work with anyone else and did not call him in my absence. On my return, I found her in the throes of an unmistakable depression, with severe insomnia, anorexia, and steady loss of weight. She readily accepted the idea of trying to deal with this emergency through pharmacological management and was immediately put on an antidepressant by the consultant we engaged. Within three weeks the somatic symptoms disappeared, her mood lifted, and she was able to resume our therapeutic explorations in a constructive manner. Because she was scheduled to leave the Chicago area to take up a prestigious academic appointment in the fall, we arranged to meet twice-weekly for the five months available to us.

This therapeutic work involved her gradual relinquishment of the idealization of her marriage as well as of the *idea* of marriage as an unalterable commitment. She came to realize that she was trying to compel her husband to remain in a situation he could not tolerate: his discomfort about their relationship had been manifest for years as a lack of interest in sexual contact. It emerged that, under the cover of acting childlike, she had actually set the tone of the marriage; her husband had tried to borrow her prestige by adopting her friends, her interests, her taste, and her standards. She realized that he was too humiliated to acknowledge that he wanted to lead a simpler, less sophisticated, more materialistic existence than she had created for them.

As she began to see more clearly that the idealized image she had constructed echoed her childhood illusions about a mother who often slipped into psychotic ideation, the patient realized that her progressive descent into childlike habits had been a desperate effort to assume the blame for any difficulties in the marital relationship or, to put this in another way, to lower herself so that she could continue to look up to her spouse. As she began to grasp that through these maneuvers she had managed to hold her husband captive – as her mother had tried to hold her captive throughout adolescence – the patient decided that it was more ethical to let him go than to adhere to her rigid prejudice against divorce.

An immediate practical consequence of this change of attitude was a marked diminution of her husband's hostility. For example, he bought her a car, which was essential for life in the community where she was to spend most of the time on her new job. Because she was also scheduled to spend several months in Europe, I provided her with the names of therapists there whom I know personally, in the hope that she would not feel abandoned upon leaving (as I assumed she had felt at the time of my vacation). By the time the end of our work approached, her depression lifted. She was looking forward to her new life with some hope – even excitement! – and she made contact with the therapist I had recommended to her. Of course, I do not know whether her improvement protected her from the possibility of later crises of depression.

Let me retrace my steps and try to spell out the therapeutic principles I followed in this reasonably successful instance of the combined psychotherapy and pharmacotherapy of an affective crisis. This disorder became manifest when the patient lost hope about restoring her marriage – or, if you will, her illusions about her principal human relationship. Because initially I did not understand the situation well enough to intervene effectively on the psychological level, nor did we have the luxury of unlimited time, we decided to use medication to reverse the distressing and dangerous physiological symptomatology. Be it noted that, although pharmacotherapy promptly increased her appetite and relieved her insomnia, the patient's despair did not disappear as long as she viewed her marital failure as a consequence of her own inadequacies. In this sense, the affective crisis was eventually ameliorated through a cognitive achievement – success in illuminating the motives for the patient's devastating self-depreciation.

How did I predict that the patient's self-esteem could in the longer run be improved through insight-oriented treatment? From the first, the patient gave me many clues to a dissociated aspect of her personality wherein she knew herself to be a very superior individual. For example, she brought me reprints of her highly esteemed writings, about which she could display unconflicted pride. The split between this healthy part of her and the pathologically impaired, dominant part of her personality had to be overcome. This therapeutic necessity turned out to be easier to accomplish than I expected, for she was quickly able to identify with my attitudes about the life of the intellect. We subsequently learned that she could not give herself full credit for her achievements in the face of her husband's overt depreciation of relatively unremunerative enterprises.

Most patients with affective disorders are much more difficult to treat than was this relatively young, extremely bright, and accomplished woman. Nor does the therapist usually start out with the ready-made idealizing transference that existed in this case as a result of the patient's admiration for my wife's intellectual accomplishments.

Let me illustrate a more typical therapeutic course, uncomplicated by pharmacological intervention, through another clinical example. This is a man whose treatment I have previously described from a totally different perspective – that of the unavoidable *failure* of a psychoanalytic effort to ameliorate a certain type of personality disorder (Gedo, 1981b, case 9). Parts of my previous account will serve well to summarize this treatment.

CASE #2

A talented actor who had tried psychotherapy on several occasions consulted me upon quitting his most recent, ineffectual psychotherapeutic experience. He had started treatment in a state of panic when his wife threw him out after she became sexually involved with their prominent attorney. Although the patient eventually adapted to the situation, he had stayed in treatment because he became obsessed by doubts. He was preoccupied with the pros and cons of cutting his losses by leaving town and starting a new life wherever his professional opportunities might be optimal, or of embarking on a campaign to restore his marriage. He had left his previous therapy because he felt he was being pressured in a dogmatic way to accept the psychiatric view of rationality. In line with a lifelong sense that he was a fraudulent person, the patient did not feel that either of his alternative programs of action authentically reflected his own wishes.

On the basis of the severity of the characterological problems, I recommended psychoanalysis, to be arranged wherever the patient decided to settle. Probably in order to keep all his options open, he then chose to remain in town and asked me to undertake responsibility for the analytic attempt. At the same time, he rescued the only child of his marriage, an 11-year-old son, from dangerous neglect by the boy's mother. He proceeded to raise the child with the intrusive overconcern that had characterized his own upbringing by what he called a "typical Jewish mother."

Actually, as we were to learn in the course of analytic work, the patient's mother was hardly typical by any standards. She lived an isolated life in a characteristic ghetto, contemptuous both of her working-class husband and the uncouth products of the American melting pot around them. She considered herself to be a member of the Russian intelligentsia, a claim her son eventually came to see as untenable, although he thought her bright enough to have fit the part. But she was not able to use her abilities to any purpose, for she was lost in the romantic haze of her girlhood in tsarist times. She had a paranoid attitude toward her neighbors' alleged envy of her status and was constantly suspicious regarding her husband's alleged propensity to be unfaithful. Although the patient had no knowledge of any philandering on his father's part, the latter certainly absented himself a great deal, especially after the birth of a second child, the patient's only sibling. This brother was six years younger than the patient but was never a serious rival for his mother's preference. As one might expect, he grew up to be much better adjusted than the patient, a sober and prosaic person like their father.

In his childhood, the patient identified completely with his mother's attitudes: he felt that he had maternal responsibilities toward his brother, he viewed his father as a villain, and he experienced the neighborhood children as inferior savages. When he started school, these attitudes provoked considerable retaliation, and he was forced to come to terms with the world of actuality through superficial compliance with social demands. It was the need to pretend that he was different from his mother that launched him on his acting career, initially by gaining acceptance as a clown and a group mascot. This uneasy compromise between the world of his mother and that of others persisted as long as he lived in the parental home. When, in his early 20s, he left to attend a famous school, he experienced confusion and panic. He was able to persevere with his training because he obtained adequate psychotherapeutic assistance. At this point, he became involved with a girl for the first time. After some initial difficulties with erectile potency, he felt more or less adequate with this depreciated person. The relationship dragged on for some years, and it was in this setting that he became preoccupied with his first interminable obsession. He felt he could not marry the girl because such a decision would kill his mother, and he was afraid to end the affair because of his conviction that this alternative would drive his mistress to suicide.

This era of confusion came to an end when the patient met his future wife. Although their relationship began because he was able to impersonate a man-of-the-world rescuing a damsel-in-distress, her wish to get married ended his obsessional indecision about his previous affair; it also ended his excessive concern about his mother. His indecisiveness began to manifest itself mostly around issues involving his career, because this was the one area of life about which his iron-willed wife had no strong opinions. She was soon undeceived about his façade of adequacy (even his sexual potency gradually disappeared over the years), and she responded to her disappointment with impotent outrage or imperious demands that he change. Until the charismatic man for whom she abandoned the patient came along, however, she was never able to take the initiative to get out of the marriage. Even at the time the analysis started, moreover, she had no interest in divorce; she took the position that she was being forced to meet her own needs as best she could, pending the requisite changes in her husband.

Following a decision to stay in Chicago, partly determined by serendipitous involvement in a TV show that proved to be very successful, the patient entered analytic treatment with me. In circumstances I shall describe shortly, this effort had to be changed to a form of therapy that cannot be classified as a psychoanalysis; altogether, my contact with the patient lasted for about eight years. When we discontinued treatment, he still wished to restore his marriage, but his character problems continued to make him unacceptable to his wife. In the meantime, he had been living with another woman whom he held in contempt and whom he was afraid to leave lest she commit suicide. The parallel to his situation during his years in school is obvious. He considered the treatment to have been a worthwhile investment because it had helped him to raise his son without committing all the errors his mother had perpetrated with him. The boy had left for college, where he was surviving better than his father could when left to his own devices. The security of the therapeutic relationship had permitted the patient to persevere with his work better than ever before, and the success of his show secured his financial position for life.

Lest these adaptive gains sound insignificant, let me go into some detail about the frightening vulnerability we uncovered early in the course of this treatment. In his chronic state of indecision, the patient begged or insisted that I give him direct advice about his various dilemmas; because I generally avoided such a nonanalytic role, he turned for assistance to his wife, who never hesitated to intervene. If she was unavailable, the patient overcame his sense of helplessness through frantic skirt-chasing, an activity for which his professional training gave him excellent preparation. It is of some interest that, in the context of his sadistic abuse of women, he seldom experienced any problem with his potency. But most of the material of his sessions was focused on his longing to restore his marital relationship with a grossly idealized version of his wife, as well as on a continuous effort to disavow the fact that she was either paranoid and overtly grandiose or severely depressed. Without the fantasy of fusion with an omniscient woman, the patient felt overwhelmed, almost literally unable to organize his behavior.

My efforts to correlate these dynamics with their presumable antecedents in the childhood past with his mother regularly met with contemptuous dismissal. In fact, in the patient's scheme of things, none of my pronouncements sounded sufficiently dogmatic or sufficiently insistent to merit serious attention. He was, however, able to grasp the fact that he wished for a magical cure and that he could not endure the humiliation of facing his actual limitations. Indeed, it was his refusal to acknowledge these limitations that had exasperated his wife to the point of leaving him.

Early in the second year of our work, the summer vacation period brought this tenuous equilibrium to a crisis point, largely because the patient's wife and I were away at the same time. By the time the patient and I resumed work, his panicky sense of needing my assistance was covered over with mistrust and arrogance. Abetted by the taunts of his wife to the effect that he had sought treatment in order to indulge his infantile propensities, he then refused to use the couch or to attempt to free associate. This decision brought the effort to use the analytic method to an end. Although he made no move to discontinue treatment or to reduce the frequency of sessions, the patient ignored my efforts to investigate the anxiety that underlay his retreat from analysis. At the same time, he began an intense search for an ongoing relationship to a woman, while he tried secretly to maintain the symbiosis with his wife. I understood this need for a heterosexual success as a defense against what he experienced as a homoerotic transference in the treatment. That a mistress was supposed to replace me as a second safety net when the symbiosis with his wife was disrupted was apparent from his choices: he initially tried a number of mental health professionals, and when he found them relatively intolerant of his peculiarities, he turned to a European scholar of an upper-class background of the kind he attributed to me. He was able to manipulate this psychologically naive girl most of the time, and eventually she agreed to keep house for him. In sexual relations, he treated her as an animate tool, and he was potent, experiencing unprecedented pleasure from these fetishistic activities.

After a couple of years of this adaptation on the basis of splitting his requirements among three need-satisfying objects, this Rube Goldberg apparatus collapsed because the girlfriend became dissatisfied with her depreciated status and temporarily left him. During my summer vacation that year, the patient abruptly developed a profound, agitated depression of alarming intensity. Within a few weeks, he lost more than 40 pounds. On my return, I thought that an emergency hospitalization might be necessary, and I immediately arranged for a consultation with a pharmacotherapist. However, the patient refused to take the prescribed medication, and within a few days of my return, his depression, with all its physiological concomitants, abruptly disappeared. Thus it became clear that the transference relationship with me had assumed a stabilizing function that prophylactically forestalled this severe affective disorder. Yet even in the patient's view there was nothing magical about this, for the function of regulating his affects within tolerable boundaries could also be provided by the self-effacing ministrations of his girlfriend, whom he soon succeeded in ensnaring again.

These circumstances probably explain the fact that neither my concern about the patient's refusal to take my verbal interventions seriously nor the evident stalemate of the treatment discouraged the patient from persevering with his daily appointments. He made it perfectly clear that he would regard any move on my part to stop seeing him as an outrageous abandonment. In effect, he demanded a cure and insisted that I provide one by complying with *his* procedures. These proved to be needed until a shift occurred in the relationship with his wife. After some years, she became disillusioned with her lover and, in desperation, offered to resume the marriage. The prospect of unremitting exposure to her arbitrary tyranny now filled the patient with dismay and temporarily impaired his illusions about her perfection. As a result of this development, it became possible for him to grasp that his negativism was a characterological attribute, an automatic reaction to the danger of losing his sense of autonomy because of his propensity for symbiotic fusion. This set of automatized behaviors had its ideational counterpart in a conviction, hitherto unconscious, that he was the only person in the world who knew the basic truth, that is, that he alone understood the impossibility of attaining reliable knowledge.

Faced with this information, I told the patient that I had no hope of influencing him through my verbal interventions. Following this consensus, we both felt free to allow our collaboration to peter out. Having secured the continuing availability of his wife and of his girlfriend by means of a series of false promises and outright lies, the patient planfully diminished the frequency of his attendance in treatment, without untoward effects, and the therapy was eventually terminated. I trust I have made clear that no remedial work was accomplished in this instance. I assume that the patient remained vulnerable to severe affective lability when left to his own devices. The treatment relationship had secured him against the occurrence of such crises – except in the midst of significant interruptions – until the general circumstances of his life made this assistance seem superfluous. With luck, he may avoid future crises. Because more than 20 years after he first consulted me his professional activities are still very much in the public eye, I know that he continues to do well, at least in that regard.

I can add that for the past 30 years I have concentrated on the psychoanalytic treatment of personality disorders, so that my clinical experience has included relatively few cases seen fewer than four times a week. Consequently, I have probably functioned as an automatic modulator of affective reactions for a number of patients in a manner homologous with my role in the foregoing treatment, without necessarily becoming aware of this fact. In the course of some of these analyses, I have had the opportunity to do remedial work concerning the missing psychological skills that these persons had to acquire in order to avoid disorganizing episodes of excitement or apathy. These interventions generally involved explanations about the patient's propensity to ignore affective signals that should serve as feedback, that efforts needed to be made to calm down (in the case of mounting excitement) or to seek greater stimulation (in that of increasing apathy). I might also mention that Galatzer-Levy (1986) reported that such interventions may, in the course of lengthy treatments, even teach some persons with *bipolar* disorder to modulate their affects so as to avoid serious mania or depression.

Lest I sound like a Pollyanna, I must also reiterate that remedial work of this kind is exceedingly difficult, time consuming, and costly: As financial support for psychological care diminishes, it is feasible for relatively few patients. It is also quite burdensome for the therapist, who cannot be blamed if he or she prefers to earn a living by choosing more rewarding professional activities. After all, one can never be certain that in a therapy of this kind a major affective crisis can be avoided, particularly if our treatment efforts induce an iatrogenic regression. That is, we are always between a rock and a hard place: if we see these patients frequently enough to become effective in a remedial sense, we may automatically set regressive forces in motion. I should like to illustrate this risk by presenting a brief summary of still another treatment, one that ended in failure because the patient could not tolerate such regressive developments.

CASE #3

A successful professional in his late 40s was referred to me for an analysis because of the exacerbation of a chronic depression. He had previously refused to undertake the pharmacotherapy recommended by another consultant, and I saw no reason to hesitate about a trial analysis. As things turned out, the patient experienced an almost instantaneous transference cure of his black mood and mild insomnia. As he put it, he felt better because a person he could respect evidently thought well of him.

The crisis that led him to seek help affected his work as well as his family life. At work, he was about to become the most senior person in his firm, and he did not feel confident about his ability to attract business as the retiring older generation had done. At home, he felt unable to satisfy his wife's emotional demands, for reasons he did not understand. She was a decent, attractive, and intelligent woman, whose only fault was a tendency to compensate herself for her husband's neglect by spending more money than was reasonable. Yet the patient had always been grossly unfaithful to her and did not enjoy their sexual life. In his frequent encounters with prostitutes, he generally enacted masochistic scenes of bondage. The actual event precipitating his depression was the decision to give up these escapades because of the increasing risks inherent in the AIDS epidemic.

The patient began his treatment by announcing that, contrary to what he had agreed to, he would not accept an analytic schedule; allegedly for business reasons, he wanted the option to shift some of his appointments with me from one day of the week to another. Because his decision created some flexibility in my schedule, his demand was at first easy enough to satisfy. The patient soon began to absent himself for brief vacations, allegedly required by his wife. After about six months of this pattern, we both realized that we were not making any headway in understanding his inner life and that the reasons he gave for avoiding a more intense treatment effort did not hold water. He agreed to begin analysis on his return from the next family vacation.

As soon as he started on a schedule of four sessions a week, the patient's sense of well-being evaporated. He reported that on his trip a minor dispute with his wife had so enraged him that he had flung a chair against the wall. Recalling this incident reminded him that he had had frequent temper tantrums as a young child; he could not recall how he managed to suppress them, but his recent outburst was unprecedented in the last 40 years! His depressive mood gradually became focused on the possibility of his having contracted an HIV infection.

When I pointed out that he could easily verify whether this fear was realistic, he reluctantly arranged to be tested but was not relieved when the tests were negative. By this time, however, *my* vacation was on the horizon, so that it seemed most likely that his barely controlled anger and his deepening black mood were caused by his sense of not being able to control our relationship. He had no awareness of the personal dimensions of this issue and talked about it in financial terms exclusively. Suddenly, this wealthy man became convinced that he could not afford the treatment.

Shortly before my departure, the patient announced that in my absence he would have to reevaluate whether he could continue in analysis; moreover, he canceled his appointments for the last week of my availability, purportedly because of a business trip. On my return, he called to say that he was on antidepressant medication because of a severe exacerbation of his mood disorder. Despite the recommendation of his pharmacotherapist that he continue his work with me, he expressed the wish to rely on medication alone. That this acute crisis was a reaction to feeling abandoned was strongly underscored by an episode that occurred on the date of my scheduled return. In a panic about the possibility of a heart attack, the patient went to an emergency room, only to be told that nothing was wrong. As I see this transaction, he could regain some sense of being in control of himself only by insisting that his physicians treat him in the manner he prescribed for them. Under the circumstances, I was forced to admit defeat.

In retrospect, my treatment plan for this person turned out to be too ambitious. Had I refrained from trying to remedy his depressive vulnerability he might well have remained stabilized in the fortunate transference constellation with which our contacts began. Although there is no assurance that he would have weathered my periodic absences if I had continued to allow him otherwise to set his own schedule, it is certainly clear that initiating the transference reenactment of aspects of his early childhood[1] brought about contingencies he was not prepared to accept for the sake of potential future benefits.

Although by itself achievement of a symbiotic transference adaptation does not ameliorate the patient's basic psychological defect, it

---

[1] The most traumatic aspect of the childhood past appeared to have been the birth of twin brothers when the patient was two years old, with a consequent relegation of the patient's care to a hired servant that led to years of ragefulness on his part.

can gradually lead to changes in actual life circumstances. These may diminish the stresses likely to overload a faulty adaptive system. This clinical illustration demonstrates that in some cases a symbiosis may not be a tenable solution to the type of dilemma I have postulated. My patient had patched over his defect through the repetitive enactment of a masochistic perversion; when the failure of this attempted adaptation forced him to seek treatment, he experienced the "holding environment" of the analysis as a cruel prison from which he felt compelled to escape. Clinicians who have therapeutic experience with addictive personalities (e.g., Khantzian, 1987) report that reliance on substance abuse is an alternative pathway available for covering over affective disturbances. Hence in our treatment ventures with persons who suffer from perversions, addictions, and other archaic syndromes, we must always be prepared for the outbreak of affective crises. The point I am trying to make here is that syndromes of this kind may serve as desperate home remedies for a lack of affective control in those persons who are unable to use human assistance to achieve such control.

Affective crises will generally drive people to seek help, but, as my clinical examples clearly show, they can also supervene as unexpected complications in the course of treatment with severe personality disorders who have previously patched over their vulnerability in this area through a variety of defensive behaviors. In crisis contingencies, pharmacotherapy may become necessary. However the crisis is overcome, restoration of affective equilibrium does not signify mastery of the underlying apraxia. Remedial treatment that would help the patient to acquire missing psychological skills generally requires the use of the psychoanalytic method, because defenses against reexperiencing archaic feeling states have to be overcome in order to come to grips with the basic defect. The intensity of the dysphoria produced by such iatrogenic regressions may exceed the patient's tolerance, so that in certain instances remedial work may not be feasible.

III

From Biology
to Clinical
Psychoanalysis

CHAPTER 7

An Epistemology of Transference

In the concluding chapters of "Studies on Hysteria" (Breuer and Freud, 1985) Freud first reported his astonishing discovery that neurotic patients, when seen in psychotherapy on a daily regimen, tend to reexperience certain aspects of their past in relation to their physician. Within a few years, Freud (1900) realized that it is the childhood past that clamors for repetition in such a transference. Moreover, he soon concluded (Freud, 1909b) that the transference consists in repeating both sides of a childhood conflict–in other words, that resistance phenomena are just as revealing about pathogenesis as are direct expressions of infantile wishes.

In 1914, when he prepared his rebuttals of the criticisms of his theories by skeptics such as Adler and Jung, Freud specified that pure "transference neuroses" could be expected to develop only in the course of analyses with patients whose childhood development had culminated in an "infantile neurosis." He concluded that, whenever the vicissitudes of early life led to alternative possibilities–the contingencies Freud then conceptualized as an excessive shift in the direction of "narcissism"–psychoanalytic treatment could not succeed, precisely because the availability of the analyst would fail to evoke infantile love and hatred and the defenses against them.

As I believe I demonstrated in my book on the history of dissidence within psychoanalysis (Gedo, 1986), the most significant clinical controversies since Freud's reformulation of his theories in the early 1920s – the revision necessitated by the realization that his initial hypotheses could not account for many forms of adaptive disorder – revolved around the issue of the appropriate treatment of cases wherein a transference neurosis either did not occur at all or, if it did manifest itself to some degree, did not constitute the most significant determinant of the pathology.

To summarize the history of these still unresolved disputes: A more conservative faction of analysts generally advocates the standardization of psychoanalytic technique, the application of stringent criteria of analyzability in patient selection, and meticulous attention to those ancillary conflicts that tilt the balance in the direction of regression from the vicissitudes of an infantile neurosis toward more archaic adaptive equilibria. This has been the position of those with more modest therapeutic ambitions, such as Freud himself (1937), later Anna Freud (1965), and the ego psychologists (e.g., Hartmann, 1964; Hartmann, Kris, and Loewenstein, 1964). In contrast, those who wished to extend the curative range of psychoanalysis beyond the transference neuroses, such as Ferenczi (1908–1933), Melanie Klein (1984), and British and American advocates of theories of object relations (e.g., Winnicott, 1958, 1965; Kohut, 1971, 1977, 1984), took up positions that represent the mirror images of the conservative ones. They broadened the scope of analyzability and permitted themselves greater freedom in altering analytic technique. At the same time, they postulated that structure formation preceding the crystalization of an infantile neurosis could have a decisive influence on pathogenesis – as Kohut (1966) put this, a separate line of development.

Depending on one's adherence to one of these alternative traditions, the clinical experience of an analyst is bound to yield widely disparate observations. Although I have always leaned toward the more radical alternative, for my analytic work has convinced me that Freud's concept of a "pure" transference neurosis is a theoretical fiction that no analysand can ever approach, in my conceptual efforts I have tried to take an ecumenical position. I am convinced that, if we refrain from deliberately tilting the course of an analysis in any specific direction, we can almost invariably elicit phenomena that support the views of both conservatives and radicals.

In response to the traditional elements of psychoanalytic technique, we will evoke some variety of a transference neurosis (see Gedo, 1981b, Epilogue); if we pay close attention to various regression-promoting factors, such a repetition of the infantile neurosis will gradually recur in clearer and clearer form. At the same time, we have the opportunity to observe the emergence of a different set of transference phenomena—a set I call "archaic transferences" (Gedo, 1977a). These are repetitions in the analytic situation of the childhood developments Freud collected under the rubric of "narcissism." Systematic analysis of "narcissistic transferences" became possible as a result of Heinz Kohut's work of the mid-1960s; unfortunately, some of his followers have tended to narrow the focus of their analytic attention to this set of transferences, thereby mirroring the reductionistic error of Freud's clinical theories before 1914. Lest we throw out the baby with the bath water, however, it is important to reiterate that transference neuroses and archaic transferences (the problems of "Guilty Man" and "Tragic Man," respectively [Kohut, 1977]) are generally to be found in almost every analysis; to put this somewhat differently, the analyst may deal with one or the other of these potentialities exclusively by means of certain technical choices and selective attention and inattention (see Gedo, 1980).

As I reviewed in chapter 3, I have tried to expand the number of alternatives by calling attention to the repetition in the analytic situation of certain primitive behaviors that do not form part of either an infantile neurosis or an archaic transference. These phenomena correspond to the manifestations of what Freud (1920) called the "repetition compulsion"—automatisms that do not necessarily involve any object relationship and certainly cannot be understood in terms of either the reality or the pleasure principle. These behaviors stem from the persistence of areas of primitive mentation that have never been encoded in symbolic terms. In the majority of instances, such activities are not pathological; they are woven into the fabric of adaptation seamlessly, as building blocks of the person's individuality, basic components of self-organization that guarantee continuity of the subjective sense of self (Stern, 1985).

In accord with the principles of the hierarchical model of mental life (Gedo and Goldberg, 1973), the several categories of repetitive transference experience I have just outlined are universally expectable in any adult capable of functioning outside of a sheltered environment.

The emergence of any of these patterns in the analytic situation as a consequence of the purposeful regression set in motion by this form of treatment is largely a matter of the acuity of a trained observer in noting the relevant phenomena. Nonetheless, the relative significance assumed by these alternative modes of functioning at any stage of an analysis is heavily influenced by certain technical choices on the part of the analyst.

To illustrate this principle, let me refer to the work of Searles, especially as reported in his most recent book (1986). Searles, whose views on this matter seem to be congruent with my own, has found that he evokes what he calls "borderline psychotic transferences" in all his analytic cases, who include dozens of colleagues! Because he has found a nonintrusive, expectant, and largely silent approach to be optimal in handling such transference developments, Searles has adopted this technical approach as his standard operating procedure in analysis. Although he does not say so explicitly, I believe that Searles's ability to evoke the primitive transferences in question is a direct consequence of this chosen technique, which maximizes the analysand's regressive potentials.

Let us contrast the technical choice advocated by Searles with the analytic technique Freud (1909b) used in the case of the Rat Man, the treatment he offered as a prototype of his work with the transference neuroses. As the excerpts from his daily notes on this case published in the *Standard Edition* (pp. 251, ff.) clearly show, Freud established an active and vigorous dialogue with his analysand, with whom he dealt at all times as a rational adult fully capable of joining in the enterprise of examining the material of his associations. I need not go beyond the reminder that when the Rat Man came to his session hungry, Freud felt free to offer him food, to substantiate the point that the treatment situation barely departed from the conventions of ordinary social intercourse. I choose this example from an era before analytic technique was standardized as a result of insight into the role of character-resistances in obstructing the emergence of regressive material in order to clarify the contrast with the technique of Searles. Eighty years ago, Freud's technique merely allowed him to gain a glimpse of the compromise formations that bound derivatives of previously repressed material that threatened to elude the censorship.

If this pair of contrasting technical approaches, separated by three generations of psychoanalytic development, strikes the reader as an artificial dichotomy, let me offer another set of examples from the contemporary psychoanalytic scene. Let us recall that Kohut (1977, 1984) ultimately decided that psychoanalysis cures not so much as a result of insight, promoted through interpretation of unconscious content, as by means of internalizations set in motion by optimally managed frustrations at the hands of an empathic (self)object. Consequently, the school of self psychology advocates a treatment technique stressing the empathic acceptance of the subjective point of view of the analysand. Given the consistent application of this approach, it would be difficult to discern any material beyond the analysand's reactions to this nurturant, structure-promoting activity on the part of the therapist. In other words, this technique is suitable only for the evocation of "selfobject transferences"; little wonder that Kohut also concluded that these are the most crucial repetitive phenomena encountered in the analytic setting! Contrast Kohut's approach with the "classical" technique of analytic traditionalists, wedded to the primacy of interpretation (i.e., the elucidation of hitherto unconscious conflicts concerning infantile wishes). How could the consistent application of such a technical prescription eventuate in the emergence of a selfobject transference? No wonder traditionalists look upon Kohut's observational data as iatrogenic artifacts! And vice versa: no wonder Kohut arrived at the conclusion that the emergence of infantile sexual wishes in the course of analysis is merely the pathological consequence of a traumatically unempathic treatment method. . .

I do not cite the self-fulfilling nature of the prophecies of both schools of thought in order to call out a plague on both houses (although they probably deserve no less!). I have outlined the circular nature of their clinical theories, treatment techniques, and the resultant observational data in order to underscore an inescapable dilemma that afflicts us all. If, as an ecumenicist, I have hedged my bets by using as complex an analytic technique as I am able to master (see Gedo, 1979a; 1988, Epilogue), thereby keeping open the possibility of eliciting the repetition of modes of functioning characteristic of numerous phases of childhood development, I have merely avoided the grossest kinds of reductionism – it is *not possible* to avoid the distorting consequences on subsequent events of whatever we do in the analytic situation.

Perhaps all that I have said thus far is actually self-evident – an application, in the field of psychoanalysis, after the passage of half a century, of Heisenberg's insight about the epistemological constraints on physical experimentation. But if it is granted that we do, indeed, labor within such constraints in making analytic observations, we must also face the inevitable inference that all of our concepts are therefore in need of thorough revision. To be sure, this task has already begun in certain quarters: consider that in 1987 the Chicago Psychoanalytic Society heard Robert Gardner present a challenging paper wherein he tried to illustrate that the context of human attachments unceasingly exerts its distorting influence on our self-inquiry.

Let me put the matter in terms of a chemical analogy: for the past century, we have operated within the assumption that our observational field was like a clean vessel through the use of which we have an opportunity to study the properties of that strange compound, the human mind. If we have recognized that we are, in fact, participant-observers – an insight long proclaimed by the interpersonalists among us[1] – we have likened our role to that of a solvent that does not react with the material we are studying. Very recently, we began to concede that the minds we observe have powerful effects on us that cannot be dismissed as mere countertransference complications; but we have thus far failed explicitly to concede that, in fact, some degree of mutual reactivity is inevitable, that we are bound to exert at least as much personal influence on the mind being observed as the observed person exerts upon us. There are no clean vessels in psychoanalysis – our observations are never about the analysand per se; they are at best about the nature of the mutual influence exerted within the analytic dyad. Analytic "neutrality" is not merely an unattainable theoretical fiction: it is also a mischievous notion that leads us into an epistemic never-never land.

To sharpen the focus of this discussion, I need to reiterate that I am not simply asserting once again that analytic observation is handicapped by the unavoidable subjectivity of the observer. That is an essential truth about the limits of our reliability, but one for which we are able to arrange scientifically acceptable controls through the use of multiple observers. It must never be forgotten that *all* our knowledge is

---

[1] In order to avoid misunderstanding, I wish to stress that I am *not* in agreement with the interpersonal school, precisely because it fails to make the necessary effort to translate the observational data obtained in the interpersonal field into hypotheses about the intraphysic world. Although this chapter highlights some elements of the actualities produced by the participants in treatment, I am trying to focus on the difficulties produced by the unpredictable variability of these factors in arriving at valid conclusions about mental dispositions.

"personal knowledge," as Polányi (1974) put it. Psychoanalysis is no different in this regard from other branches of science. Our field does differ from all others because our very presence as observers drastically alters the data we are attempting to apprehend.

What are the logical consequences for our views on transference phenomena if we accept that psychoanalytic data gathering is inevitably skewed by the qualities of the observer–subject transaction? Clearly, what requires revision is not the manifest content of what we have observed over the past century in the psychoanalytic situation. Rather, we have to abandon the assumption that the behaviors in question are manifestations of the analysand's mental dispositions in pure culture. Instead, we must view them as products of a system of mutual-feedback mechanisms. This means that, if we wish to draw valid conclusions about the "subject" of our observations, we have to assign a certain valence to the input of the observer. For the moment, I do not believe we are adequately prepared to accomplish this task, but it may not be too early to list some of the accumulated clinical experience that has a bearing upon it.

Let me begin by noting the inconsistency of our usual position about the sex of the analyst as a cogent factor in the treatment process. On one hand, we all seem to believe that the analyst is a screen blank enough to provide any analysand with an adequate surface upon which the gamut of his or her potential transferences may be projected. I certainly know this to be true in my own case. Yet few of us seem to have the courage of our convictions about this matter, for in referring patients to an analyst – particularly a second or third analyst – we tend to give some thought to their special needs for a person of one sex or the other. So the truth seems to fall somewhere in the middle: the analyst's sex does not generally preclude the development of transferences repeating transactions with a person of the other sex, but the actuality of the analyst's person does seem to have a certain weight in evoking those transferences for which he or she is, so to speak, "typecast."

Although very little has been written about the subject, the issue of "typecasting" seems to apply to the analyst's age as well. Shortly before he died, Gitelson (personal communication) called for some thoughtful attention to this issue, but I do not believe it has ever been addressed. As I get older, I seem to find it easier to evoke grandparent transferences than used to be the case; I also have the impression that it has become a rarity for me to be experienced transferentially as a sibling figure. But I can make the same point much more confidently from a slightly different perspective: one can scarcely avoid pouring fuel on the fires of a potential for idealization as one gets older and more prominent as a psychoanalytic author and educator. Contrast the actualities confronted by the patients of such a "Guide to the Perplexed" with those presented to the potential analysands of young candidates – how hard those patients must work to create the stuff out of which an idealizing transference is woven!

To turn from these unalterable and obtrusive facts about the analyst's actual person to issues of greater subtlety, I believe the degree to which the participants in the analytic dyad share a single cultural matrix has a tremendous bearing on the ease – or difficulty – of recapturing the analysand's relations with the early childhood milieu. Some years ago, I reviewed my analytic experience in this regard (Gedo, 1979b) and was surprised to discover that I had had startlingly less success with people from certain subcultures than with the rest of my clientele: specifically, I had little luck with analysands of southern background and with those whose parents were European immigrants of peasant stock. Not only are both subcultures relatively unfamiliar to me, I am afraid I may have approached analysands from these backgrounds with certain prejudices the nature of which never became clear to either of us.

The other side of this same coin is represented by the fact that, no matter how carefully we intend to maintain our analytic anonymity, we have no way of concealing what we know, what we believe, who we are. I do not mean that it is obvious to our patients whether we voted for Harold or Fast Eddie,[2] or neither! It is much more difficult not to reveal our commitments to high culture or professional football, to free enterprise or current fashion. The very selection of magazines in our waiting rooms reveals important things about us, as do the clothes we wear, the holidays we choose to observe, the furnishings we provide for our office, or the professional books we keep – and do not keep – on our shelves. Of course, these are only external manifestations of "who we are" – but by that token they are relatively easy to discuss.

More direct evidence about the specifics of our inner world is externalized by means of our language, including its paraverbal aspects. Some years ago, I asserted (Gedo, 1984, chap. 8) that analytic success is

---

[2] Recent candidates for the office of Mayor of Chicago.

contingent on the development of a "shared language" between the participants, a viewpoint I still believe to be valid. However, here I wish to call attention to the other side of the coin – namely, to the fact that however we may try to keep a low linguistic profile, our verbal communications remain as unalterably individual as the "voice" that carries them. Not only are our vocabulary and idioms as personal as our fingerprints, our very syntax, however "correct" it may be, betrays our innermost being through the choices that characterize our rhetoric. Did those of my analysands whose forebears were members of an oppressed peasantry hear the language of their exploiters in my incompletely Americanized *façon de parler?* How many of my readers would succumb to the temptation to ape the aristocrats of a Tolstoy novel by lapsing into French at such a juncture as this? But I can assure you that I came by this affectation honestly, not alone by reading highbrow literature, but by following the manners of my admired grandfathers, including their penchant for such books. I know that these ways are no longer acceptable to everyone, but I can no more dispense with them than I can lose my accent.

Although most aspects of our language are unalterable, we do, of course, possess some degree of latitude about the manner in which we communicate with our analysands (see Gedo, 1984, chap. 9). The laconic style that gradually gained currency as *the* classical technique of analysis clearly provides less intimacy than many otherwise analyzable patients can bear and promotes the rapid emergence of negative transferences referable to the earliest phases of development – as the recent exposé of psychoanalysis by a writer whom it literally drove to drink poignantly demonstrated. It is true, of course, that in these matters there do exist circumstances in which less is more, but that self-evident truth does not mean that we may assume that more is necessarily less. It behooves us to think through at every turn what effects the form as well as the content of our discourse may produce on the analysand.

I am convinced that the nature of the transference (or sequence of transferences) we evoke is strongly influenced not only by the *extent* of our verbal participation in the analytic dialogue – it is also influenced to a similar degree by a number of other choices we make in encoding our messages. As I have emphasized on a number of occasions (Gedo, 1981b, p. 291; 1988, p. 218), one of the most important of these concerns the degree to which we infuse our communications with the affect appropriate to our words. Obviously, this choice is simultaneously contingent on decisions about whether or not to engage in a direct dialogue, as though one were one of the characters on the stage that is the psychoanalytic setting, whether to provide the patient with opportunities to cushion the impact of our message by making clear that our affectivity is under total control, and so on. At any rate, the more direct and affect-laden our communications are, the more likely they are to tilt the analytic relationship in the direction of transferences of relatively archaic origin. Interpretations offered in a really dispassionate manner or in a formal style, especially if we introduce conceptual issues as we explain ourselves, call upon our patients to exercise secondary-process capacities – even those for abstract thought – only available in midlatency of even later.

At the other end of the spectrum of communicative possibilities, resort to the language of posture and gesture, to wordless vocalizations, such as moans, growls, laughter, grunts of skepticism, astonishment, or contempt, to the whistling or humming of familiar tunes, pushes the analysand in the direction of earlier modes of relatedness and the transferences attendant thereon. As I reviewed in chapter 1, Levin (1991) has shown that a predominant use of metaphors straddles the gap between the foregoing communicative styles. I suggest that such a compromise between primary- and secondary-process thought may optimally evoke oedipal transferences.

We could elaborate the fascinating technical vistas opened up by these and similar considerations about the rhetorical dimensions of analytic activity; but I have already given enough examples suggesting that the analyst's language plays an important role in determining the development of specific transferences to make it more desirable to move on to more general and fundamental issues. If the actualities of the analyst's age and sex, sociocultural background and language, and a host of less obvious components of identity can skew the nature of the transferences he or she can evoke, not to speak again of the effects of technical choices dictated by theoretical preconceptions, what are the implications of these sobering facts for our views on psychopathology and on the formation of character?

I believe we have consensus about differentiating a psychoanalytic nosology from one based on other than analytic premises on the grounds that personality assessment should focus on the individual's propensity to form specific transference types. One of the early statements of this viewpoint was Zetzel's (1968) important paper distinguishing those "hysterics" whose symptomatology reflects the conflicts of an infantile neurosis from others, with essentially the same manifest behaviors, whose hysteroid characteristics screen problems of an archaic nature. In his initial statements about what he then called "narcissistic disturbances," Kohut (1971) similarly cautioned against basing personality diagnoses on phenomenology; he insisted that only the unfolding of the transference could reveal whether a person suffered from oedipal or narcissistic pathology. My own recent book on psychopathology (Gedo, 1988) carries this stress even further: I assert that diagnostic predictions cannot reliably be made on the basis of any time-limited sample of behavior or extraanalytic observations, not only with regard to oedipal versus narcissistic problems, but also for the gamut of functional possibilities.

What are the consequences for a nosology tied to the sequential development of transferences in the analytic situation of the conclusion that the specific transferences evoked in psychoanalysis are codetermined by the analyst's technical convictions and his or her actual characteristics as a person and a personality, beyond any issues involving unresolved problems on his or her part (cf. Kantrowitz et al., 1990)? Such a view compels us to confine our diagnostic schemata to statements about the emergence of a series of transference positions in the context of particular analytic circumstances. To give only the most obvious of illustrations: if, in an analytic situation conducted in accord with the "classical" technique–that is, one wherein the analyst's interventions are truly confined to interpreting unconscious material and an attitude of expectant neutrality otherwise prevails–there develops an archaic transference of passionate intensity, with recurrent crises whenever the analysis is interrupted, even briefly, we can only conclude that we have evoked a "borderline psychotic transference," as Searles (1986) calls this; it is not legitimate to postulate that such a contingency is a marker of a "borderline syndrome." The same analysand, if actively provided a "holding environment," as Modell (1984) advocates in certain cases, might well respond with the formation of an idealizing transference. And *that* development would not justify making a diagnosis of a narcissistic disturbance. And so forth.

It is precisely considerations of this nature that have led me to conclude that an optimally conducted analysis should permit the analysand to relive as many kinds of transferences referable to all phases of early development as possible. To facilitate insight into these dispositions and to permit their gradual resolution by means of interpretation, it is generally convenient if they emerge for analytic processing more or less sequentially, one by one. If the transition from one type of transference to another is to be made feasible, the analyst's contribution to this dyadic shift must be to alter the analytic situation whenever the previously established status quo has outlived its usefulness. One dimension along which such shifts may be made is the hierarchy of therapeutic modalities that Goldberg and I (1973) appended to our developmental model of mental functioning.

I later elaborated this schema (Gedo, 1979a), stressing that analytic technique has always encouraged shifts from interpreting, either to confining our activities to the role of an empathic witness or to more active measures, "beyond interpretation," designed to lend patients psychological expertise. Here I must reiterate that the hierarchical schema Goldberg and I devised almost 20 years ago was deliberately skeletal: its five-stage rendering of development was arbitrary, intended to encourage hierarchical conceptualization by offering relative simplicity. The schema is too coarse to differentiate the profusion of transference possibilities from each other; consequently, it also cannot pretend to offer any therapeutic prescription about the analytic posture most appropriate to evoke particular transferences. It merely provides one gross indicator of the directions we may follow in that quest.

Perhaps the time has come to conclude this chapter by returning to our starting point. Psychoanalysis is best characterized as that science of mental life which is built on the observation and understanding of the ever-recurrent cycles of repetition in human behavior. Our standard observational setting is the psychoanalytic situation, and the analysand's repetitive behaviors in that context are called transferences. Because we impose a dyadic transaction on our data gathering, most of the transferences we have the opportunity to observe necessarily reproduce ways of relating to others in the past, particularly in childhood. In order to reenact these old transactions, the analysand needs the compliance of the analyst – if not as an actor restaging the old script, at least as a willing puppet to whom the necessary roles might be attributed. The ever-shifting consequences of these complex cybernetic mechanisms have generally been mistaken for static internal conditions characteristic of the analysand. Systematic correction of the resultant misconceptions is an enormous task awaiting the next generation of psychoanalysts.

CHAPTER 8

· ———————————— ·

The Psychoanalytic Paradigm and Its Alternatives

istorically, we have tended to define psychoanalysis-as-a-treatment-method, differentiated from psychotherapies informed by psychoanalytic principles and hypotheses, in terms of sets of technical instructions conveyed to the participants as early as possible in the transaction. There has been little change in these since Freud standardized his procedure, sometime between his work with the Rat man and the publication of his "Papers on Technique" (1911-1915) three or four years later.

Psychoanalysis, for most of us, is still that technical approach which calls upon the analysand to associate freely in a setting calculated to minimize external stimulation and tilt the focus of attention in the direction of introspection; in parallel, it directs the analyst to attend in a "freely hovering" manner and to articulate interventions only insofar as these overcome impediments to the process of free associative self-observation and/or they draw novel conclusions from them about the analysand's mental universe. To be sure, as Eissler (1953) was the first to codify, most patients require additional assistance of various sorts in order to keep the analytic process moving on the road to fresh insights and the changes in psychic organization these may ultimately make possible. The articulation of such "parameters," and of the specific modes of mental functioning that make it necessary to introduce them, has constituted the major thrust of my own conceptual work in psychoanalysis for the past two decades (see Gedo, 1979a, 1981b, 1984, 1988; Gedo and Goldberg, 1973). For the purpose of differentiating psychoanalysis proper from analytically informed psychotherapies, however, the appropriate introduction of these measures "beyond interpretation" does not constitute a decisive distinction. As Eissler made clear, these measures easily fit into the analytic technical armamentarium, provided that the specific rationale for the use of each parametric intervention is ultimately made explicit to the analysand, as the initial step in curtailing its occurrence.

There is less agreement about another aspect of the psychoanalytic situation, that of promoting therapeutic continuity and emotional intensity by arranging to meet as frequently as the analyst's schedule (or, alas, various irreducible constraints on the analysand) will permit. As a result of such continuity, internal equilibrium is generally shifted in a direction unfavorable for the defensive apparatus; that is, the more uninterrupted the analytic work is, the more it is likely to promote a therapeutic regression in those people whose personality organization recommends the trial of the analytic method. Persons in whom potential regression stirs up anxiety about the possibility of disintegration – and, a fortiori, those who do actually undergo disorganization in regressive situations – are likely to respond to such a trial with emergency defensive maneuvers or even flights from treatment. Hence, some analysts using relatively loose criteria in patient selection seem to believe that regression-promoting measures, including scheduling sessions at maximal frequency, are best avoided.

In my own clinical experience (Gedo, 1984, chap. 2), I have found that the dangers of regressive developments are generally overestimated and can almost always be overcome by timely measures "beyond interpretation" that make it possible to persevere with an analytic effort.[1] At the same time, I have found that less intensive forms of therapy have very little chance of permanently altering profound disturbances in personality organization. In other words, I cannot agree that in therapeutic matters "less is more." Despite these findings, I hesitate to differentiate psychoanalysis from other therapies on the

---

[1] I have described an exception that may prove this rule as Case #3 in chapter 6, this volume.

basis of frequency of sessions alone, for it is widely known that "psychologically minded" patients, particularly those who have had previous experiences in analysis, can often engage in analytic work on relatively sparse schedules. (Of course, it is also clear that nonanalytic therapies may be conducted on an intense, even daily basis, sometimes for good and sufficient reasons.)

In his celebrated correspondence with Groddeck, Freud (1977) tried to sum up the theme of this discussion by stating that a psychoanalyst can be identified by virtue of his attentiveness to issues of transference and resistance. Of course, this aphorism preceded the development of psychotherapies based on analytic theory that, at the same time, try to avoid falling into "wild analysis." In the wake of the American triumph of ego psychology, psychoanalytically oriented psychotherapists are seldom guilty of overlooking resistances, and they are more likely to postulate the occurrence of transferences on the basis of insufficient evidence than they are prone to *miss* transference developments. Even a generation ago, Tarachow (1963), among others, pointed out that the actual difference between analysis and analytic therapies is that in analysis proper we tend to encourage the transferences to flower, unless and until they become major resistances, whereas in psychotherapies we generally nip them in the bud by interpreting them more expeditiously! (See also Gill, 1983a.)

Although I believe Tarachow's didactic distinction to be largely valid, I also know that it is honored more in the breach than in the observance. At any rate, it is not simply the therapist's intentions that determine the course of transference developments. To paraphrase the Renaissance surgeon Ambroise Paré, we may tend to the patient, but only nature can cure him. We do know that the most successful analyses are characterized by the successive emergence of affect-laden transferences, each of which proves at length to constitute the crucial resistance to the reliving of some of the others. Whenever in the process of being mastered and assimilated, major insights about enduring patterns of mental organization yield novel developments in the transference arena, we are tempted to conclude that an "analytic process" is unrolling, like an oriental scroll. In contrast, many psychotherapies focus in a more limited manner on one transference constellation, or perhaps the alternation of a set of two transferences.

Some 40 years ago, Felix Deutsch (1949) outlined a specific technique to bring about these "sector analyses." Yet the manifest techniques of traditional psychoanalysis may also be used to effect such circumscribed therapeutic aims. To illustrate, when Kohut (1977) advocated the termination of treatment with certain analysands suffering from severe impairments whenever workable "compensatory structures" have become operative, he abandoned the accepted aim of psychoanalysis to illuminate the full extent of the analysand's inner life. In this sense, the portion of analytic work performed in accord with Kohut's recommendations corresponds to a "sector analysis" as this was conceived by Deutsch. We might do well to define a treatment as analysis if and when a *full* program of exploration has been carried out, without concerning ourselves obsessively with the specific methods employed to reach that goal.

On the other hand, this viewpoint implies the corollary judgment that any transaction that precludes the achievement of unfettered self-inquiry transforms a treatment into something other than psychoanalysis. It is this conviction that renders so many among us excessively cautious about abandoning a purely interpretive stance in psychoanalytic work, despite the results of follow-up studies (Erle, 1979; Erle and Goldberg, 1984) showing that far fewer than half the cases that reach a mutually agreed upon termination can be handled in such a puristic manner. In my experience, noninterpretive interventions, the rationales of which are explicit in the course of the work, seldom, if ever, preclude the exploration of all aspects of the analysand's inner life, including the emergence and resolution of transferences referable to all developmental phases.

As a matter of fact, on the basis of my activities as a clinician and as a consultant and supervisor, I have come to the conclusion that the single most important factor impeding full exploration of the psyche is the rigid application of any preconceived conceptual schema to the clinical material. Perhaps, in fact, it would be more accurate to say that the doctrinaire misapplication of any of the perfectly serviceable clinical theories at our disposal will bring actual exploration of the analysand's individuality to a halt. On one hand, the specific theory pushed by the analyst may be truly ill suited for the organization of any particular analysand's clinical data; on the other–a circumstance perhaps more frequent because most of our clinical theories do apply to some extent to just about everyone–the truths revealed by a restricted range of interpretations are bound to become organized as effective resistances to the emergence of other painful issues that lie beyond these defined boundaries.

I do not mean to imply that any of us should be capable of conducting an analysis without resort to preexisting theoretical schemata, in a never-never-land of pure inductivism. But, as Charcot used to tell Freud, "La théorie, c'est bon, mais ça n'empêche pas d'exister" – theory is good, but it does not stop things from existing, especially things beyond the matters it was intended to explain. And even if a deductive interpretation should happen to be on the mark, it will often lead to bewilderment instead of insight if it does not fit the clinical material tightly and in convincing detail. It is, of course, even more of a problem if such seemingly arbitrary pronouncements are accepted in a spirit of fearful submission or expansive idealization.

I suspect that what I have just stated may be acceptable to most as a description of adequate microtechnique in psychoanalysis: we don't shoot off our mouths 'til we can see the whites of their eyes. If I have taken the trouble to state what I hope will seem obvious, I have done so to emphasize that the gamut of technical features that are generally said to characterize psychoanalysis proper – the free associative method, the frequency of sessions, meticulous attention to defensive operations prior to "id analysis," the tendency to allow transferences to blossom before interfering with them by interpretation – and other aspects of "the gold of analysis" (to quote Freud once again) have the common aim of permitting the interpretation of clinical data on a more detailed, particularized, and immediate basis.

Do I mean to claim that as psychotherapists we are condemned to engage in deductive guesswork, in a formulaic and arbitrary manner? Not at all; in fact, no more than we are forced to fall into these undesirable habits in our psychoanalytic guise. I believe that if we wish to avoid these manifestations of a contemporary technique of pressure, suggestion, or even hypnosis, when we do not see patients on a daily basis, have no systematic access to free associative material, and lack the "red thread" of the unrolling transferences to guide us, we are forced to restrict our interventions to those matters about which we may draw conclusions through direct observation in the consulting room. In psychotherapy we do well to worry less about the hermeneutics of the patient's mental contents and concentrate instead on the overt deficiencies of his psychological performance, deficits I designate as apraxias (Gedo, 1988).

Of course, I believe that the identification of apraxias is an important task in psychoanalysis as well; in fact, every intervention "beyond interpretation" should be designed to compensate for an apraxia on the part of the analysand, on the way to helping him acquire the requisite psychological skill. Some years ago, it was customary to divide the task of filling in a patient's apraxias from other aspects of the curative process by initiating treatment through a period of "ego building" psychotherapy, which was explicitly regarded as a "preparation for analysis" (see Rappaport, 1960). Because it was felt that the activities required to teach patients new psychological skills might make it very difficult later for the analyst to be the kind of "blank screen" that was supposed to encourage the development of interpretable transferences, it was generally regarded as desirable to transfer such patients to another analyst when it was deemed possible to begin the analytic work proper. Nowadays, most of us no longer believe that we can ever approximate blankness, so that the practice of having different therapists for the various phases of the work seems to have fallen into disuse.

My own experience in initiating psychoanalytic treatment with patients whose personalities do not seem suitable according to the usual criteria has led me to conclude that permitting such patients to borrow missing skills through explicit instruction (what Samuel Ritvo privately termed "lend-an-ego" in the analysis of children) does not interfere with the subsequent development of transferences. Such an intervention, if indicated, constitutes one aspect of a transaction the analysand will experience as an archaic transference, the repetition of early childhood situations of learning by identification. If the archaic transference is then accurately interpreted, it will no more interfere with the emergence of other transferences than do other forms of repetition.

But, on balance, an analysis remains a hermeneutic enterprise; in contrast, in most psychotherapies the task of detecting the nuances of the patient's meanings proves to be insurmountable. I suspect that it was this technical problem, especially prominent in the difficult cases he was considering, that led Kohut (1984) to underplay the role of insight even in psychoanalytic work, in favor of stressing the importance of empathy. In this matter, as in that of sector analyses, I view Kohut's ultimate preferences as a tilt in the direction of analytically oriented psychotherapy.

Yet I trust that I have made it clear that I consider the gradient from a purely interpretive technique, hypothetically feasible only in the analytic setting, to a technique exclusively concerned with the repair of apraxias and dyspraxias, likely to be necessitated only in treating patients too impaired to be analyzable, to constitute a continuum. In the middle of this range, whether, retrospectively, we designate a treatment as a psychoanalysis or as something else is completely arbitrary. That is why I am less concerned about how my technical innovations are classified (albeit I regard them as solidly within "psychoanalysis proper") than I am concerned about whether they are rational proposals, designed to deal with the full complexity of mental functioning. (I shall return to this issue in chapter 9.)

For those who are uneasy with waffling in classification, I should like to offer another suggestion. Perhaps we can avoid the blurring of the boundaries of psychoanalysis if we do not make our judgments on the basis of the activities of the participants in the treatment transaction but focus instead on the nature of the ongoing process between them. However that process has been produced, we may be justified in calling it analytic if, on the whole, it does not turn out to be circular; if neither participant interrupts it before the other is content to do so, if it does prove to have a beginning, a middle, and a natural ending; if it is free to explore the full range of mental activities (however distressing this may be for either party); and if both analyst and patient experience termination as a parting without unfulfilled obligations. A tall order, but perhaps justified as an ideal toward which we may aspire.

To recapitulate my thesis thus far, I see insight-promoting psychotherapy and psychoanalysis as phases within a continuous spectrum— entities that can be differentiated only on the basis of arbitrary criteria. They are based on a unitary psychoanalytic theory of mental functioning and development, in comparison with which nonpsychoanalytic theories of the mind may be seen as naive or reductionistic.

Let me now turn to some more specific issues I should like to single out for discussion. First, I want to focus on a matter pertaining to the theory of psychoanalytic technique—namely, to endorse the point of view that the analytic procedure transcends the decoding of the analysand's communications and the reconstruction of the history of the latter's inner life. In implicit agreement with the claim I have put forward for many years, L. Friedman (1988) endorses as legitimate an additional goal of analytic activity—that of acting upon the analysand in some manner designed to promote better adaptation. He designates such measures as the activities of the "therapist as operator"; I (Gedo, 1988) took them into account by describing psychoanalysis as "a technology of instruction." I entitled a book *Beyond Interpretation* (1979a) to emphasize the point that a great deal of the analyst's activity is neither hermeneutic nor a matter of historicism.

Friedman demonstrates that a great deal of the discomfort felt by an analyst/therapist alert to the actualities of his work is caused by the seeming absence from our theories of any acknowledgment of therapeutic intentions. He appears to believe that the analyst is thereby placed in an inherent paradox: he or she must promote improved adaptation while disavowing any intent to do so. I have some reservations about accepting this view. When I look back on my own experience as an analytic patient, I am convinced that no such paradox confronted my analyst, for the goal of improving my adaptation was indubitably my own. This aim was sometimes promoted by measures on the part of the analyst that today I would classify as "beyond interpretation," but by rendering such assistance (for example, in decreasing unserviceable levels of anxiety through the use of humor) these operations did not imply that the transaction was fueled by the analyst's therapeutic needs. I submit that whenever the analysand clearly understands the desirability of making adaptive changes and the progress of treatment has assumed priority among his goals, the analyst as facilitator of the necessary learning or mastery is merely fulfilling the responsibilities undertaken as part of the explicit therapeutic compact. In the case of psychoanalysis proper, it is well for this compact to specify that the analyst's agenda for change will always be confined to whatever the patient desires.

The paradox Friedman has discerned arises only with patients whose desire to get well is undercut by compulsive behaviors under the sway of the repetition compulsion. To illustrate, I once attempted to help a person who always literally ran away from intense human transactions. When, before initiating the analysis, I asked her what we might do if she were inclined to run from me, she gravely told me that it would then be my duty to block her path to the door. Less than a year later, when, in a great huff, she started to walk out on me, I made a beeline for the door, in accord with her instructions. With an expression of infinite malice, she told me that if I dared to touch her, she would call the police. I was then in the dilemma highlighted by Friedman. In that instance, I resolved it by bowing – I trust gracefully! – to the priority of the analysand's immediate freedom of action. I offer this illustration not to recount the therapeutic outcome, but to focus on the fact that the analyst can always be guided by the patient's current *instructions* about what the latter expects, always within the boundaries of the rationally possible and therapeutically legitimate, to be sure. In other words, I see the dilemma not in terms of a paradox for the analyst but as a consequence of the externalization of the patient's mutually opposing, uncoordinated motivational systems. When these are made accessible to the analysand's self-reflection, a reasoned decision about what is desired can generally be made.

I should now like to turn to another issue, one that constitutes probably my most serious disagreement with the prevailing analytic consensus. I have in mind an assumption, seemingly shared by a sizable majority of practitioners, that a psychotherapy grounded in psychoanalytic theories and making use of the information accumulated through a century of psychoanalytic practice should, of necessity, strive to come as close as possible in its aim and techniques to those of psychoanalysis proper. Much of the literature (see L. Friedman, 1988) discusses only those therapies intended to promote better adaptation by means of insight. One might say, as a corollary, that such treatments rely, for the most part, on the interpretation of transference constellations that emerge in the therapeutic situation; in order to facilitate these developments, they encourage the use of as much free association as possible by the patient and of a stance of ideal neutrality by the therapist.

In contrast to these views, I believe that psychoanalytic theories of mind, of personality development, and of therapeutics should permit us to devise a broad array of therapeutic modalities for rational application in various contingencies. Fully 25 years ago, I published (Gedo, 1964) a proposed classification of the principal models of treatment based on analytic premises in common use at that time. That paper was inspired by the prior work of Grinker and collaborators (1959) and of Tarachow (1963) in the realm of defining therapies that do not take the achievement of fresh insight as their principal goal. Obviously, I cannot claim any priority for the views I am espousing; on the other hand, I do not think that I am articulating an idiosyncratic viewpoint either.

To illustrate the kind of modalities of treatment I consider to be "psychoanalytic" without being "insight directed," let me once again cite some of the work of Kohut. As most readers will recall, Kohut (1984) came to believe, on the basis of his efforts to treat so-called narcissistic personality disorders by means of analysis, that beneficial therapeutic results seemed to follow not so much upon the analysand's acquisition of valid self-knowledge; but on the provision of an empathic ambiance. (In Lawrence Friedman's terms, Kohut recommended tilting the therapeutic prescription decisively in the direction of the therapist as a direct influence, at the expense of hermeneutics and historicism.) When Kohut's followers, the self-styled self psychologists, applied this formulation in psychotherapeutic settings that did not claim to be psychoanalyses, a type of treatment eventuated that attempted to supply a putative emotional need on the part of everyone in order to provide what we loosely term "support." Whatever we may think of the validity of Kohut's views about empathy, they constituted a serious hypothesis based on psychoanalytic experience, so that the therapies devised with their help are based on one analytic atlas of the mind, although they do not use insight as a primary tool.

If I may approach the same matter from a different perspective, I would question unstated acceptance of the hypothesis of one particular school of thought within psychoanalysis, that of those who conceive of all maladaptive phenomena as consequences of conflict. This view fails even to acknowledge the possibility of psychopathology as a result of some kind of deficit. I find this viewpoint particularly inadequate in view of the gradual assimilation by psychoanalysis of many Piagetian ideas, including that of the centrality of learning for personality development. From such a perspective, useful psychotherapies might be devised that would take advantage of certain transference constellations to promote identifications with the therapist (or other avenues of instruction) without providing insight from either the dynamic or the genetic point of view.

From the vantage point of three decades of full-time clinical experience in performing psychoanalyses, I have come to expect better results from therapies that follow more modest programs of this kind than from those that are aimed at achieving psychoanalytic results without the maximal therapeutic resources of a full-scale analytic situation. I have been particularly impressed (both in my own clinical work and in assessing that of others) with the likelihood that therapies focused on achieving insight in nonanalytic settings are likely to bog down in an unceasing round of shifting transference reactions, each of which serves as a very efficient resistance to the elucidation of any of the others. I am fully aware, of course, of the practical obstacles that may compel us, in particular cases, to compromise our best judgment about what ought to be done; but in an ideal world, when would one recommend "insight therapy" in preference to psychoanalysis proper?

Let me turn my question on its head: in his therapeutic work with children, Winnicott (1965) preferred to do as little as possible, provided his interventions would "unhitch the developmental catch" that stood in the way of the child's progress. If psychoanalysis is not feasible, why is the provision of insight necessary to restore an individual to some acceptable path through the life-course? And if something simpler and briefer might do, are the risks attendant on permitting transferences to flower really justified? Or, to be even more radical in my skepticism, if we seldom succeed in arriving at valid insights when we see analytic patients five times a week, how can we expect to do so in other settings?

CHAPTER 9

· ───────────────────────── ·

Clinical Evidence as the Basis of Analytic Theory and Modifications of Analytic Technique

As I mentioned in the previous chapter, the standard technique ideally used in performing psychoanalysis crystalized before Freud (1909b) published the case of the Rat Man – probably, in fact, in the middle of that very treatment, when Freud decided to refrain from asking the patient to focus his associations on key elements of the material. Although in the 80 years that followed various modifications have been proposed – for instance "active techniques" recommended by Ferenczi (1925) shortly after World War I – these have invariably been rejected by the vast majority of analysts, so much so that it is no exaggeration to claim that psychoanalysis as a form of therapy is definable in terms of adherence to a definite set of procedures. This conclusion is of vital importance for every aspect of the discipline, for it has been rightly pointed out in various quarters that all branches of psychoanalytic theory must be based on clinical evidence obtained in the psychoanalytic situation.

The nature of that situation may be defined in terms of the analytic "setting" (Winnicott, 1954) and of treatment technique. Although effective techniques dealing with the bewildering range of clinical contingencies had not been previously codified, Eissler (1953) apparently solved the resultant conceptual quandary when he proposed to designate interpretation as the characteristic therapeutic tool of psycho-analysis and to call all other necessary interventions "parameters," the rationale for which must be understood (and eventually conveyed to the analysand) if the treatment is to qualify as a psychoanalysis. The simplicity of this ingenious suggestion has had an irresistible appeal. At the same time, its acceptance has led to a tendency to look upon the use of parameters with disfavor, as if they represented a contamination of the pure gold of analysis with the copper of therapeutic compromise.[1] Voices have also been raised to point out that noninterpretive interventions are de facto ubiquitous (see Gill, 1979), an observation with which I am in emphatic agreement (Gedo, 1981a).

Another way to describe this source of confusion is to note that Eissler's definition of a parameter is so vague as to be meaningless: it hinges on the alleged *necessity* of any noninterpretive intervention. In the heat of any clinical encounter, determination of such a necessity must remain a matter of judgment. Even on paper, there are theoretical disagreements on this score. A more conservative school of thought advocates maximal caution about the introduction of potentially super-fluous parameters: that school of thought suspects that these departures from a purely interpretive stance are probably consequences of the analyst's countertransference problems and possibly expressions of unresolved characterological pathology. On the other side, efforts have been made (see Gedo and Goldberg, 1973; Gedo, 1979a) to specify the types of maladaptive personality structure that call for the rational use of specific kinds of interventions "beyond interpretation." Needless to say, conservatives are seldom ready to diagnose a structural deficiency. Instead, they suspect the operation of defensive regression, unless adherence to an exclusively interpretive technique (which they tend to equate with "psychoanalysis") has led to a therapeutic disaster.

As I have stated elsewhere (Gedo, 1988, Epilogue), I view interpre-tation itself as one type of intervention intended to overcome a psy-chological deficit, in this sense no different from parametric interven-tions designed to deal with apraxias of other kinds. Interpretation is

---

[1] Some traditionalists who possess an inquisitorial streak take the attitude that any failure in analysis is most likely to have been caused by some impurity in applying the standard technique of interpretation in a setting of "neutrality." This amounts to the transformation of analysis into a sacred ritual—as we know, such measures are unfailing because their disappointing results are invariably attributed to the shortcom-ings of those who performed them.

necessary only because the analysand is unable to process his or her own free associations. Gardner (1983) has persuasively argued that the standard technique of analysis should consist in assisting analysands to arrive at their own interpretations. If we accept this cogent conception, we may look upon all analytic interventions, including interpretations, as efforts to help patients to learn hitherto missing psychological skills—a view congruent with the biological evidence summarized in chapter 1.

At any rate, from a pragmatic point of view, I believe that the dangers of "nonintervention" (i.e., of scrupulous adherence to a purely interpretive technique) are much greater than are those of intervening needlessly in some noninterpretive manner. Whenever the differential diagnosis between dyspraxic repetition and apraxia is unclear, I advocate a therapeutic trial of offering the analysand something that may relieve apraxic bewilderment. Should such an intrusion into the patient's inner world prove to be unwarranted, it will ultimately produce rage, negativism, a temporary clinical impasse, symptomatic relapse, or worse. It is true that on the way to such pathognomonic evidence that the intervention was superfluous there may be a period of false compliance, but any temptation to claim therapeutic gains on that basis soon leads to dramatic developments of the unfavorable sort I have listed. If we refrain from permanently closing off patients' associations, evidence will soon surface (perhaps in the form of dreams or dramatic enactments) indicating that interventions have been inappropriate—or insufficient! In either case, we are then in a good position to explain the proper rationale of our analytic conduct, as Eissler (1953) advocates.

Clearly, my technical bias may give aid and comfort to analysts who wish to enact authoritarian characterological propensities or irrational countertransference attitudes of inappropriate "helpfulness." However, in the hands of such impaired analysts, no particular technical prescription is likely to work: after all, even their manifest adherence to an exclusively interpretive strategy could only constitute a reaction formation that would, in practice, fail to counteract the underlying problem. To put this in a more traditional manner, my technical recommendations are likely to prove effective only if noninterpretive measures are offered in the same spirit of analytic neutrality that is required to make effective interpretations.

To recapitulate, it should not be difficult to ascertain the extent to which noninterpretive measures are helpful and truly necessary in the course of analytic work. As I have already stated, when we neglect to offer *needed* assistance of that kind, our insistence on a technical approach predicated on dealing exclusively with unconscious intrapsychic conflicts can only lead to therapeutic failure. (These results were clearly documented in Firestein's 1978 report on terminated analyses conducted in accord with that approach, a matter I discussed in detail at the time [Gedo, 1980].) It is pertinent to recall in this connection that, in a study of the actual practices of well-regarded analysts throughout the United States, Erle and Goldberg (1984) found that fewer than one-third of attempted analyses could be terminated without significant, explicit departures from a purely interpretive technique. I assume that unnoticed variations in technique are even more frequent.

Whenever the "classical" technique of psychoanalysis is applied without modifications to nonneurotic disorders, such an extrapolation from the original rationale (unheard of until recent years except for some of Ferenczi's experiments before World War I, the failure of which delimited the proper range of "analyzability") amounts to an unwarranted leap of faith. I believe it is an irrational procedure, as the results of numerous outcome studies have demonstrated. To cite only the most recent of these (Wallerstein,1986a), the Menninger research comparing the "psychoanalytic" approach to character disorders with one employing an admixture of nonanalytic measures, the use of the purely interpretive technique with patients handicapped by structural deficits yielded decidedly inferior results (see also Kantrowitz, Katz, and Paolitto, 1990).

Actually, there is a fair degree of consensus about the kind of therapeutic technique best employed in various clinical contingencies. Thus, I have never been challenged about my resort to extensive parameters with the patients I have described (with the single exception of a Kleinian critique by Segal and Britton, 1981).[2] An important current of opinion, however, seems to prefer classifying the kind of work I advocate as something other than "psychoanalysis" (see Wallerstein, 1986b; Dewald, 1981), although some of this group are willing to grant

---

[2] Kleinians claim that they are able to deal with all contingencies by means of interpretation alone, a view predicated on their unreasoning belief in the operation of symbolically encoded fantasies in earliest infancy. In my judgment, their arbitrary "interpretations" produce therapeutic results despite a lack of validity, in the manner postulated by Glover (1931).

that variations are to some degree unavoidable as concomitants of the "art of psychoanalysis" (see Richards, 1981). Although it is tempting to refrain from arguing about such a semantic quibble (and I have sometimes stated that I have no preference in the matter [Gedo, 1984, pp. 33–34]), I have come to the conclusion that it would be mischievous to do so, because psychoanalysts share a consensus that only data collected in the psychoanalytic situation are centrally relevant for our theory construction. In other words, conceding that noninterpretive measures render a treatment nonanalytic would risk the exclusion of a body of vitally relevant clinical evidence from the purview of the discipline.[3] It seems to me that scientific progress in psychoanalysis depends on applying exactly the same criteria to the evaluation of new hypotheses that we use to validate older ones. It is no more legitimate to imply that innovative technical proposals are evident manifestations of irrationality on the part of their proponents than it would be to suggest that adherence to interpretive techniques alone is motivated by personal irrationalities. The *burden* of proof is on neither one side nor the other. Hence it is illegitimate to claim, as did Jaffe (1984), that good results obtained by means of noninterpretive techniques are any more likely to amount to mere "transference cures" than are similar results when they are reached through traditional methods. Such facile assumptions blithely disregard extensive clinical accounts (e.g., Gedo, 1979a, chaps. 4, 6, 8; 1984, chaps. 4, 5) that show the emergence and resolution of a sequence of intense transferences despite frequent resort to noninterpretive techniques.[4]

---

[3] Silverman and Silverman (1983), in a review sympathetic to new technical proposals, take exception to the evidential value of case reports that fail to provide "verbatim accounts" of the transaction and imply that only access to the primary data (via recordings) can satisfy scientific requirements. Although such records are indeed vitally needed for validation studies, an individual practitioner's clinical experience does have some degree of evidential value for the purpose of developing new hypotheses. Moreover, hypotheses gain influence within the psychoanalytic community not because they are ultimately validated (which may or may not happen) but because they acquire plausibility for a significant number of fellow practitioners on the basis of the latters' personal experience as therapists (as well as analysands!). To induce them to try novel technical proposals, we must present them with compelling narratives of analyses carried out in these new ways. Ultimately, of course, validation studies of the kind advocated by the Silvermans will take place only if researchers are similarly convinced that new hypotheses are persuasive enough to merit serious study.

[4] Many respected commentators have, of course, accepted my proposals as legiti-

As a matter of fact, comparable studies of the course of analyses conducted in the traditional manner (Erle, 1979; Erle and Goldberg, 1984; Kantrowitz, 1987) and in accord with modalities that include the planful use of noninterpretive methods (Gedo, 1979b; 1984, chap. 2) are now available. In terms of process criteria (i.e., the attainment of a mutually agreed upon termination), the technique that moves flexibly between interpreting and using measures "beyond interpretation" permits the successful conclusion of a much higher proportion of analyses.[5] In other words, analyses are much more likely to fail because we adhere to inappropriate technical orthodoxy than they tend to be ruined by excessive noninterpretive activity, if that activity is chosen on a rational basis. Whenever I have erred in selecting such interventions, the worst that has followed has been that the analysand felt depreciated until I detected that reaction and we succeeded in determining its sources: grist for the analytic mill!

If it is granted that, in view of the foregoing, one version of psychoanalysis has as valid a claim to that designation as any other, we are confronted by the fact (first mentioned by Robert Michels in an unpublished 1974 discussion of *Models of the Mind* [Gedo and Goldberg, 1973]) that the expansion of psychoanalytic theory represented by the hierarchical model of mental life is bound to alter profoundly the nature of the data we collect in the psychoanalytic situation. This is true not only because the hierarchic view does not narrow the observer's focus of attention to derivatives of any specific phase of development, but also because the resultant expansion of technique tends to evoke a different sequence of transferences from that produced by the "classical" method of analysis. (The implications of this tendency to alter our data base depending on the analyst's activities and even his or her qualities as a person were discussed from an epistemological viewpoint in chapter 7.)

To be more precise, traditional technique steers analyses in the direction of the flowering of a transference neurosis and therefore will

---

mately psychoanalytic (see Modell, 1974; Kaplan, 1981; McLaughlin, 1983; Gill, 1981, 1983b; Rangell, 1981; Rodgers, 1990).

[5] Those who are tempted to attribute this higher rate of success to my personal merits as a clinician (as if those were different from the usefulness of the theory of technique I espouse) should be reminded that these superior results are matched by the work of candidates I have supervised and other analysts who have chosen to consult me about their work.

highlight data referrable to such an entity: guilt conflicts, castration anxiety, the inhibition of ambitions and aggression, introversion, and the elaboration of fantasy life. Although such material is plentiful in analyses conducted in accord with my recommendations as well, the transference neurosis often occupies a much narrower segment of such analyses, which generally focus at least to the same degree on more archaic transference constellations. Contrary to the claims of hostile critics such as D. Goldberg (1984), close attention to archaic material does *not* imply that the intrapsychic conflicts of more advanced sectors of the personality will not be (or even cannot be!) interpreted. As a matter of fact, in my experience, interpretation of such conflicts is greatly facilitated by prior interventions designed to correct the analysand's structural deficits.

In view of these radical changes, expectable with regard to the analytic process if it is conducted in accord with my proposals, the shock expressed about these recommendations by certain conservative commentators is not out of place. When Reed (1985) writes that my techniques go beyond analysis (as she knows it) to "cure" people, she is perfectly right. In L. Friedman's terms (discussed in chapter 8), I am quite candid in espousing the role of the "analyst as operator." D. Goldberg (1984), though confused about certain details of my work, correctly sees it *in toto* as an effort to change the very definition of psychoanalysis. But the issue worth pondering is the one raised by Wallerstein (1986b): if traditional analytic methods are relatively ineffective beyond the boundaries of the transference neuroses, what is the rationale for recommending even a modified psychoanalytic approach to deal with other personality disorders? Or, as Wallerstein put it, what is wrong with psychotherapy?

I have every reason to believe that in asking that question Wallerstein had in mind psychotherapies grounded in internally consistent psychoanalytic premises. Indeed, there is nothing the matter with psychotherapy of that kind—but the work I have tried to promote has wider scope and greater ambitions than such therapies generally possess. To begin with, I advocate use of the standard psychoanalytic setting, including the greatest frequency of sessions feasible.[6] On one

---

[6] In my own practice, this has meant five sessions per week, with negligible exceptions when extraneous circumstances compelled me to compromise this standard for relatively brief periods.

hand, this frequency is necessary to provide an adequate "holding environment" (Modell, 1976) for those patients who cannot remain in adaptive equilibrium when left to their own devices; such persons are often so traumatized by any interruption in a daily analytic schedule that they need one or more treatment sessions just to recover from such a disruption. In other words, to make proper use of any therapy, these patients should not be subjected to more than one hiatus in treatment per week. On the other hand, insofar as the crucial pathogenic events of a patient's life have been partially transcended through the erection of more or less successful, albeit maladaptive, defensive operations, in order to promote a better solution of the problem, it is necessary to set in motion an iatrogenic regression. This requirement is best met by a maximal frequency of sessions, as well as the other regression-inducing features of an analytic setting, like the analysand's recumbent posture, the exclusion of external stimuli, and the like.

Beyond the question of setting, the technique I recommend makes use of the method of free association and its complement, "evenly hovering attention" on the part of the analyst—the hallmarks of a genuine psychoanalytic situation. It is this aspect of treatment that makes possible the shift from a topical arrangement of therapeutic discourse (i.e., one that is focused on events and problems) to one linked in accord with emotionally meaningful patterns, the crucial process we call the emergence of transferences in the face of endopsychic resistance. It will be recalled that Freud (1977) chose to define psychoanalysis as the therapy that is focused on the elucidation of transference and resistance.[7] Whatever one's preferred definition may be, it is the opportunity to elucidate the effects of the past upon the present (i.e., transferences), largely by means of interpretations and reconstructions, that produces change in the maladaptive, dyspraxic habit patterns that constitute a major segment of the psychopathology we are called upon to alter.

I believe these statements about the basics of psychoanalytic tech-

---

[7] It is the relative neglect of the problem of endopsychic resistance on the part of Melanie Klein and her followers—the seeming dismissal of "ego analysis" in favor of directly naming putative id contents—that has made it impossible to integrate Kleinian conclusions about the archaic psyche with those of other psychoanalytic investigators (see Gedo, 1986, chap. 6).

nique are noncontroversial. It is because of my adherence to these principles that my case reports impress a reader as traditional as Rangell (1981) as relatively conventional. My techniques remind Wallerstein of "psychotherapy" because I have highlighted clinical contingencies wherein the foregoing "basics" have to be supplemented by measures beyond interpretation – if you will, with the "parameters" of Eissler's 1953 proposal – because, in addition to dyspraxias, our patients are all too often beset by structural deficiencies. These are the missing psychological skills I call "apraxias" (Gedo, 1988).

Wallerstein did not challenge my claim to have expanded the purview of psychoanalysis because he is skeptical about the evidential value of my clinical reports – he was, in fact, explicit about our agreement on that score, in opposition to traditionalists like Dewald (1981). Dewald argued zealously that only data obtained by use of traditional psychoanalytic technique need to be accounted for. Actually, Dewald's argument was circular: because the data thus obtained are reasonably well handled in terms of previously accepted theories, he saw no need for theoretical revision (which he tended to equate with the rejection of "established knowledge"); because he was satisfied with the theory of technique in past use, he continued to generate only the kind of data accommodated by his theory. Dewald was able to adhere to this schema only because he took the nonscientific position that psychoanalytic theory can be mere metaphor (p. 195); by implication, he also abandoned the need for theoretical coherence. It is ironic that an author who demands so little of himself from an epistemological point of view should try to discredit others on the narrowest grounds of scientific method!

From a methodological viewpoint, the proper solution of the problem of clinical evidence in psychoanalysis is the correlation of specific observational data with the precise therapeutic interventions that produced them, whatever the analyst's theoretical views may happen to be. Such studies will require not only primary data (as Silverman and Silverman demanded in 1983), but sophisticated statistical methodologies (see P. Gedo, 1988). Only through methods of true scientific rigor can psychoanalysis meet challenges like that of Grünbaum (1984), who faults all the evidence at our command. In the meantime, it behooves us to refrain from excommunicating each other on the ground of controversial technical differences.

CHAPTER 10

·———————————————·

The Therapeutic Results of Psychoanalysis: Outcome and Technique

About a dozen years ago, when I believed myself to be in midcareer as a psychoanalyst, I published a synoptic account of my psychoanalytic clinical activities (Gedo, 1979b); several years later, when my cumulative experience surpassed a total of 50 consecutive terminated cases, I brought my account up to date (Gedo, 1984, chap.. 2). Both reports included essential demographic data, estimates of the nature and extent of the adaptive difficulties, the duration of treatment, and the results at termination in terms of both process criteria and those of therapeutic outcome. I also discussed putative reasons for analytic failures and certain limitations in the results obtained even in cases I considered to have ended successfully.

In the spring of 1987, I decided no longer to undertake fresh psychoanalytic responsibilities, so that I am now in a position to report on the experience of my entire career as a psychoanalytic clinician, a span approaching 35 years.[1] I believe this is worth doing, despite the

---

[1] At this writing, I am continuing to work with four patients: the last person who entered analysis with me (early in 1987), and three others who have been in treatment for very long periods and show a strong reluctance to risk terminating. In none of these efforts is there any reason to anticipate surprises of a kind that would alter the conclusions I am about to set forth here.

fact that, both demographically and in terms of the kinds of problems I have dealt with, the nature of my clientele has not changed too significantly since my first report. Given the essential homogeneity of my practice through the years, it is all the more meaningful that the results in the cases I have terminated since 1983, when I wrote my second account, are clearly more satisfactory than those I reported on earlier, especially with regard to outcome criteria.

I should like to begin by stating that since I first began to do psychoanalysis, I have assayed the method with 62 individual patients; four of these persons – includes two patients whom I am still treating – have had two periods of analysis with me. Over the years, the proportion of cases that were terminated by mutual consent has not fluctuated significantly: in 1979, it was 77.8% (28 out of 36); in 1984, 80% (40 out of 50); for the most recent years, it is 77% (10 out of 13).[2] It is in qualitative terms that I discern better results, not in terms of process criteria.

My recent clientele has included a greater proportion of mental health professionals (at the expense of academics and housewives) because throughout this period I served as a Training Analyst; it is arguable that would-be psychoanalysts may possess greater adaptive resources than did the kind of people they displaced from my practice. However, this shift was relatively minor (from 25% to 30% to 40%), and analysands who were mental health professionals did not differ from those who were not, either in their psychopathology, the duration of analysis, other demographic criteria, or even their exposure to previous treatment. I have also kept the criteria for my patient selection constant.

The only other change in my clientele was the gradual but steady decline in the proportion of women in analysis with me (from 52% before 1984 to 26.7% since), a decline I attribute to the societal influence of feminism. It is certainly conceivable that I obtain better results with male patients, but I never had that impression, and most of the unequivocal analytic failures I have participated in have been with

---

[2] These figures exclude the four ongoing analyses. The percentages for earlier years are slightly inflated because the two patients who are currently in their second analyses are counted as having terminated by mutual consent at the conclusion of the first period of treatment. If they are excluded, the figure for successful termination is 76%, essentially identical to the one for the more recent period.

men. Incidentally, younger female colleagues have not shared the prejudice of their "sisters" and have often consulted me about their women patients, some of whom insisted on seeing a female analyst! *C'est la guerre* . . . .

At any rate, I believe the crucial variable in accounting for the differences I shall describe was the gradual evolution of my psychoanalytic technique in accord with the theories I have set forth since 1973 (see esp. Gedo, 1979a; 1981b; 1984, sec. III; 1988, Epilogue). Although my therapeutic procedure began to diverge from accepted traditions more than 20 years ago, my initial ventures "beyond interpretation" were relatively modest, as the case reports in my 1979(a) book (chaps. 4, 6, and 8) demonstrate. In the past decade, my technical innovations have been bolder, as I have become convinced that much of the psychopathology we have to ameliorate is attributable to apraxic defects and not solely to the repetition of dyspraxic patterns of behavior (see Gedo, 1988). The fruits of the technical experiments I have instituted are visible in the therapeutic results of the 13 analyses I have concluded since 1984. As I have stated previously (1984, p. 33), such an application of newly acquired skill and knowledge *is* what we mean when we speak of the value of clinical "experience."

Needless to say, these improved results are manifest mostly in the 10 analyses brought to a satisfactory termination.[3] In my previous reports, I have emphasized that analysands who terminated by mutual consent almost invariably improved their "work" performance, and this outcome was certainly present in all 10 of these cases. In several instances, these adaptive gains included the achievement of creativity in areas previously inaccessible to the patients – such accomplishments as publishing books or scientific articles, organizing art exhibitions, and prominently participating in public musical performances. Two patients applied their creativity in the sphere of business and attained real distinction in their early 30s. These outcomes were particularly notable because seven of these patients had sought analysis at least in part because of severe dissatisfaction with their vocational adjustment.

It is easier to demonstrate the superior results in this series of cases

---

[3] It should be noted that one of these was the reanalysis of a patient who obtained quite a good result after a previous period of analytic treatment with me but who decided to resume the work because certain illusions about her intimates continued to interfere with her family relationships.

with regard to their object relationships, which improved even more than their work adaptation: seven patients made satisfactory marriages (only one of these was a first marriage!), one turned from homosexuality to a heterosexual adjustment, and one was able to consolidate what had started out as a very shaky marital life; the last patient was (and remained) a Roman Catholic priest. These results are notably better than the ones I reported in 1984: as far as I knew at that time, only 16 out of 28 patients unattached at termination had been able to make satisfactory object choices, and several patients (mostly female) compromised by settling for a frustrating marriage or for *de facto* celibacy. I am unable to predict, of course, how long the excellent results in my recently terminated cohort of analysands may last, but I have had some posttermination follow-up with nine patients, and can report that the improvement has in all cases persisted for some time.

These outcomes deserve to be noted because, at the time they initiated analytic treatment with me, every patient in this series suffered from severe psychopathology of a kind that a short generation ago would have dictated a decision against attempting a psychoanalysis. The student with severe hypochondriasis and hydrophobia whom I describe in chapter 4 was one of these analysands and illustrates the kind of personality disturbance represented in this sample. Other patients from this series I have previously discussed are a homosexual academic afflicted with grandiosity (Gedo, 1983, chap. 5) and a man with a volcanic temperament and a propensity for sadomasochistic transactions (Gedo, 1988, chap. 1). Perhaps I can best characterize this group by stating that in only one case out of the ten was the problem focused on issues from the oedipal period (albeit such issues played an important role in each)—and even in that exceptional instance a negative oedipal fixation was in large measure the result of severe preexisting anal seduction.

If the successfully terminated analyses represent the mastery of truly challenging problems, the three cases that were prematurely interrupted exemplify that, in slightly different and more unfavorable circumstances, roughly similar problems can become insurmountable. On two previous occasions (Gedo, 1981b, chap. 3; 1984, chap. 7), I reviewed the limits of my therapeutic effectiveness, by citing material from six analyses that underscored the nature of the boundaries within which I was able to function successfully. One of these constraints was the occurrence of regressive episodes necessitating the use of a sheltered environment; another was the emergence of previously covert delusions in the course of the uncovering work; the last border I described was the inevitability of delinquent enactments within the analytic setting. As the analysts of children have long known, analytic work also cannot succeed if the analysand is symbiotically enmeshed with someone in the milieu who is adamantly opposed to treatment.

In chapter 6, I summarized the failed analysis of a man who became panicked by the iatrogenic regression evoked when he began to attend treatment four times a week; this was one of the three interrupted treatments in my series. It should be noted that I recommended the analytic method on the basis of misinformation as a result of seriously delinquent behavior on the patient's part: he had failed to inform me (or the consultant who referred him) about a major masochistic perversion, often acted out with prostitutes. I will not claim that, in itself, this information would have altered my treatment plan, but its concealment certainly raises the possibility that still more serious indicators of psychopathology, in the form of unintegrated nuclei of mentation, may have been present. At any rate, it is entirely possible that the unmanageable regressive episode would not have arisen if my period of vacation had not been scheduled so soon after we had instituted an analytic process.

The second of the cases interrupted prematurely was a person who imperceptibly lapsed into alcoholism when his (quasi-psychotic) symbiosis with his aged mother was disrupted by the onset of her senility and the necessity to sell the family home she had occupied. Once again, the regressive behavior came to a head during one of my vacations, although, in this instance, the crisis came about after several years of treatment. The patient's internist was consulted and insisted on referring him to a messianic specialist in the treatment of alcoholism, one committed to the reductionist view that alcohol abuse is a constitutionally based somatic illness. This individual met the patient's need for a symbiotic tie to a delusional person. On my return from vacation, I was met by the analysand's apologetic announcement that "on doctor's orders" he was forced "temporarily" to interrupt the work with me. Need I add that this transaction repeated certain childhood events wherein the psychotic mother drove a wedge between the patient and his father. My efforts to make such an interpretation did not penetrate the patient's alcoholic haze. It seems unlikely that the analysis would have been disrupted had the acute crisis been handled by a physician prepared to cooperate with an analyst.

The last analytic failure in this group came about without any crisis of regression: a very anxious, infantile woman married to a wealthy alcoholic was simply unable to oppose his insistence, rationalized on financial grounds but pretty clearly motivated by his envy of her positive transference experience, that she cut the frequency of her visits to a bare minimum. She did not dare to risk a marital break-up by persevering with her analysis. It is not irrelevant that the patient was a product of a slum environment and had been severely abused as a child; her husband's disregard of her needs echoed her mother's refusal to heed the child's complaints when she was sexually molested by members of the family.

It is also worth looking at the patients who continue their seemingly interminable analyses with me, two of whom, as I stated before, had had previous periods of treatment terminated by what I believed to be mutual consent but actually secretly perpetuated through the fantasy of a special connectedness between us. Not even counting their prior experiences of analysis, these patients are currently in their seventh, eighth, and ninth year of treatment, respectively. This concentration of stalemated cases in my current practice is one obvious consequence of my policy of winding up my analytic responsibilities through attrition: patients able to conclude their treatment in timely fashion have long since terminated. I believe that this inference is supported by the fact that, among the 38 persons who attempted analysis with me prior to 1984, only two remained in treatment for as long as eight years.

One of the persons who needed such a long period of analysis earlier in my career stopped her treatment after exactly 10 years, with the conscious knowledge that it could have gone on forever. She has kept in more or less steady contact with me ever since. We have now known each other for well nigh three decades, and she continues to make good use of whatever I can help her to learn in our consultations.[4]

---

[4] My interventions are now aimed at overcoming her apraxias. I am confident that if I had been willing to help her in this way when we started our work together, the outcome would have been more satisfactory. However, this woman was so impaired

The second patient whose analysis was essentially interminable (also described in my 1988 book [pp. 158–60]) persisted in it for 11 years. She made a heroic effort to improve her adaptation and persuaded herself that she could terminate, a judgment with which I had no reason to disagree. This woman also kept in touch with me for various reasons, but she contrived to do so in nonprofessional settings, where I could not behave as her analyst. In these contexts, her feelings about me (and the analysis) suddenly turned virulently negative. I have some reason to believe that this paranoid attitude permits her to maintain her adaptive gains.

As these prior experiences with analytic stalemates indicate, certain patients are able to make good use of the transference relationship during analysis to meet a symbiotic need, thereby achieving considerable adaptive improvements. If the apraxias that necessitate such reliance on external assistance are not eliminated through remedial measures, the treatment of such patients remains interminable. One of my current patients faced with this dilemma – one who attempted to terminate a first analysis years ago, only to have to resume treatment when faced with new adaptive demands – has articulated the problem quite explicitly: He is reluctant to try terminating because he knows that I will probably be unavailable if he needs assistance in the future.[5]

Of the three patients who remain in this kind of suspension, two suffer from arrests of development in archaic modes of personality organization (see Gedo, 1988, chap. 4, where one of these analysands is briefly described [pp. 66–67]); the other is incapacitated when on his own by covert thought disorders that he generally manages to disavow in everyday life. All three are sons of psychotic mothers;[6] the thought-disordered man identified with his mother's mode of thinking, while

---

at the time that I cannot assert that a definitive termination could have been reached. (This treatment is described in Gedo, 1988, pp. 25–28.)

[5] This man has been in touch with one therapist or another for about 40 years. The analyst he used before he came to me died quite some time ago. The patient is now approaching the age of 60 and is unwilling to contemplate still another switch to a fresh analyst. This reluctance has its transference implications, to be sure. At the same time, the patient has had a very distinguished career, and he has some right to maintain his dignity vis-à-vis strangers.

[6] Identification with a psychotic mother, which leads to a propensity for delusional thinking, was also the unresolved problem with the analysand who became paranoid about me after "termination."

the other two – in their effort to avoid that fate – became impervious to all outside influence, thereby impairing their further development. In all these analyses, we are now articulating these issues, with unpredictable consequences. *Qui vivra, verra . . . .*

Looking back over my analytic practice of the past three decades and more, it is apparent that my work lends itself to classification into several reasonably well-defined periods. One might call these: first, an apprenticeship of 6 or 7 years; second, a period of independent work along conventional lines that lasted for about 4 or 5 years; third, a time of experimentation, for about a decade; and the recent work I summarized in the first part of this chapter, which, I trust, might be called a period of maturity. It may be fruitful to consider the differences in the outcome of the analyses I conducted in these four stages of my career – more instructive, in fact, than any attempt I could make to compare my results with others reported in the literature.[7]

When I did not use my own past work as the standard of comparison, the claim that my technical innovations yielded better results than did traditional methods was often dismissed with the devastating flattery that I was a more talented therapist than those represented in the published surveys. I tried, feebly I suppose, to rebut these arguments by asserting that I was able to teach my methods to supervisees, whose results (based on process criteria) approximate my own. That thesis will not wash, however, in terms of therapeutic outcome, about which a supervisor has little information. Under the circumstances, my earlier work has to serve as the control for the evaluation of my recent results.

The psychoanalytic training I received in Chicago (from 1956 to 1961) was impeccably traditional, particularly because my own analysis was performed by Maxwell Gitelson, the leader of the local opposition to the heterodoxy advocated by Franz Alexander. The analyses I conducted under supervision or began independently during my apprenticeship were carried out in the spirit best exemplified by the most thoughtful discussion of technical issues from that era, Stone's (1965) *The Psychoanalytic Situation*. I tried very hard to make interpreta-

---

[7] For instance, the reports from the Boston Psychoanalytic Institute by Kantrowitz and her collaborators (1987, Kantrowitz et al., 1990) or the earlier ones by Firestein (1978) or Erle (1979; Erle and Goldberg, 1984).

tions on the basis of convincing clinical evidence, preferably within the transference, and avoided cliches taken from the literature.

This conscientiousness was rewarded by good results: at least 75% of my patients persevered with their analyses until we agreed to terminate. I put this somewhat fuzzily, because one analysand who interrupted treatment at the very point when the idea of a possible termination first came up was probably much closer to finishing than I realized, and my judgment (in 1979) to list this analysis as incomplete was not entirely sound. Not too long ago, about 20 years after I had lost touch with her, I encountered the patient at a funeral. She apologized for having been so hostile (within the transference) and recounted that she had done quite well without any further treatment. Clearly, it is just as possible to underestimate therapeutic results as to be too sanguine about them![8]

What actually distinguishes the group of patients whom I treated in the earliest period of my analytic activity from the ones I have treated since is that none of them ever came back to see me professionally after termination, whether they were content with the outcome of the analysis or, as one man told me in the very last session, they were disappointed in it. I suspect that this circumstance was a consequence of an erroneous conviction on my part that, to "work through" separation from the libidinal objects the analyst represented in the transference, it would be advantageous to give up the relationship altogether, "cold turkey," as addicts would put it. Despite this doctrinaire policy, I did subsequently hear from or about a few of these analysands. An internist I know reported, some 20 years after termination, that my very first analytic patient had extolled the benefits of her treatment, although she had never fulfilled her wish to get married; an acquaintance who was the neighbor of another analysand (who left treatment prematurely) later told me that the patient's characterological problems continued to haunt her. Whatever information I did get consisted of relatively insignificant snippets of this kind. The only finding I am able to report that is truly relevant is that during these early years I never felt any confidence about the therapeutic outcome even in my "successful" cases. Perhaps the first time I sensed that an analysis

---

[8] This is one of the startling conclusions of the research team led by Kantrowitz (Kantrowitz et al., 1990).

would have a decisively beneficial result was at the early stages of the period that followed, when the last of the analyses I had started in the first phase were coming to termination. Indeed, in the clearest instance of that kind, the analyst of another member of my patient's family later told me that my former analysand was doing very well.

I know a great deal more about the later destinies of 12 patients I worked with in the period of the consolidation of my independence as a clinician. The analytic failures I observed in this era were in cases whose regressive propensities truly forestalled analyzability; in contrast, in my earlier work, they seemed to be functions of my inexperience (Gedo, 1981b, pp. 62–62, 64–68; 1988, pp. 50–52). In the 10 cases that came to termination, the Oedipus complex in its manifold permutations had been thoroughly illuminated, and in at least half of these I felt very confident about the future value of these insights–a confidence validated by the patients' subsequent communications. One analysis was stopped prematurely for financial reasons and later had to be resumed; the second effort, conducted in accord with my later convictions, ended satisfactorily. The 10-year-long analysis that I described earlier in this chapter was also concluded during these years. About one patient I have heard nothing.

The posttermination course of the other two analysands reveals the limitations of analytic work principally focused on libidinal and aggressive conflicts. One patient became very successful as a poet and novelist as a result of her analytic gains (see Gedo, 1983, chap. 4); however, she proved to be allergic to such prosperity and returned for consultation because of her severe anxiety. Because she had left Chicago, I referred her for further analysis in her new place of residence. She has continued to communicate with me from time to time and has steadfastly asserted that the issues in her reanalysis were different from the ones we had properly dealt with. The second analyst has discreetly indicated as much. As a result of our work, the other patient had been able to get out of a marriage that kept her in masochistic bondage; she had also been quite obese and was still trying to lose weight at termination. Just recently, I encountered a good friend of hers who told me that the patient died in a traffic accident some years ago. This person also informed me that my ex-patient's life had been one of continuous unhappiness about her intractable weight problem, that she had made a second unsatisfactory marriage, and that she had tried a series of unhelpful psychotherapies. Clearly, the analysis had not dealt with certain vital issues.

It would be misleading to imply that my experimentation with methods "beyond interpretation" began abruptly. It would be more correct to say that it gradually gathered steam in the era of high excitement within the Chicago psychoanalytic community generated by the controversies around the work of Heinz Kohut (i.e., in the late 1960s and early 1970s). Indeed, I would be hard put to differentiate the effects of Kohut's influence on my work early in this next period from those of my own ideas. Whatever I learned from that source, however, was in place in my repertory by the time I published *Models of the Mind* (Gedo and Goldberg, 1973). The next half a dozen years were occupied with further modifications of technique on the basis of the hierarchical schema put forward in that work.

At any rate, I concluded 20 analyses during this third period, 14 of which were terminated by mutual consent.[9] One attempt had to be scaled back to a psychotherapy because the patient was too anxious about the potential disruption of her marriage were our work to succeed. The four analyses in which we failed altogether showed the combination of delinquency and thought disorder I have discussed in connection with my more recent interrupted cases (for accounts of these cases, see Gedo, 1981b, pp. 68–77; 1984, pp. 114, 116–122; 1988, pp. 61–65; this volume, chap. 6). One analysis was abruptly interrupted as a result of a transference enactment in which passively suffered early abandonments were actively inflicted on the analyst (see Gedo, 1981b, pp. 165–71; 1988, pp. 161–62). The patient later returned just long enough to permit us to reach consensus about the meaning of the enactment. Recently, she called me from the airport after an interval of more than a decade: she had done extremely well in every way and attributed this success (in laymen's terms, of course) to the repair of her apraxia about relying on her (intact) reality sense – a piece of learning she attributed to the manner in which I had been able to maintain my view of reality when she had subjected it to unceasing attack as she was disrupting the treatment.

---

[9] I have published extensive accounts of five of these analyses (Gedo, 1979a, chaps. 4, 6, and 8; 1984, chaps. 4 and 5) and briefer summaries about several others (in Gedo, 1981b, 1983, 1984, 1988).

I have continued to receive a great deal of information about the subsequent course of the remaining 14 patients (many of them, after all, are members of the local mental health community). One person has had a second period of analysis with me in the more recent era of my working life; two others have come back for shorter series of consultations about family crises – contacts that enabled me to ascertain that they had generally maintained their analytic gains.

The least favorable outcome was that of the 11-year treatment I have already mentioned: this divorcee has not been able to resume close relations with men, and she remains furious about her disappointment in me. Two other female patients have stayed in frustrating marriages, and another divorcee has chosen to remain celibate. One man was, after termination, unexpectedly abandoned by his wife. When he returned to discuss this, we agreed that I had been remiss in letting the "sleeping dog" of his passivity in the marriage lie. Subsequently, however, this man made a satisfactory second marriage.

It is precisely the kind of limitation in making a satisfactory adaptation in the sphere of intimacy that I have intimated about the five analysands just mentioned that has been overcome in the successfully terminated analyses I have conducted more recently. Obviously, the requisite personality characteristics developed in the later group of analysands not because I dealt any differently with their conflicts in the realms of love and hate. My technique has changed in only one way: I now pay much closer attention to the lacunae in the analysand's repertory of psychological skills. When I detect apraxias, I bring them to my patients' attention (however mortifying such confrontations may be), and I try very hard to induce them to learn what they need to know. *Ça marche!*

IV

Psychoanalysis and
Contemporaneity

CHAPTER 11

· —————————————— ·

Self Psychology:
A Post-Kohutian View

The task of evaluating Kohut's self psychology more than five years after his death is particularly difficult for me, because I happened to have been Kohut's earliest adherent as well as the person he looked upon as the first apostate from his cause. Heinz never mastered his sense of betrayal as a result of my inability to become his disciple; this unspoken reproach was conveyed only in the tears of his widow when I belatedly offered her my condolences. Gallantly, she said that the rupture was not anyone's fault, "It could not be helped." And she asked me whether I had any idea of how much I had meant to her husband. Yes, I did.

De mortuis nil nisi bene. I wish I could confine this chapter to the testimony that, in my view, Kohut's personal contribution to psychoanalysis was so important that in the past two decades all pioneering work in the field deserves to be called "post-Kohutian." Of course, I said as much at the celebration honoring Heinz on his 60th birthday (see Gedo, 1975a). For many years now, my own intellectual work has invariably focused on the specifics of the complex disagreements between us (see Gedo and Goldberg, 1973, chap. 5; Gedo, 1979a, pp. 29–31, 165–67, 176–78, 181, 209–210, 220–21; 1980; 1981b, chaps 4–7; 1984, chap. 10; 1986, chaps. 7 and 8). The failure of contributors to the literature of self psychology to take note of this extended critique has not made it easier for me to maintain a dispassionate attitude about these difficult matters.

Of course, I could place the emphasis on the other side of the coin: the invitation to contribute a chapter to a volume of commentaries on self psychology (Detrick and Detrick, 1989) should constitute sufficient acknowledgment that I have given Kohut's contribution careful thought. Indeed, I have remained on excellent terms with some of the leading contributors to self psychology, so that I know that many of Kohut's present-day adherents in fact share some of my unfavorable opinions about various discrete aspects of Kohut's heterogeneous writings or the practices prevalent within the movement he founded. I can therefore empathize with the need of certain members of an embattled minority to ignore those who question the truth of its cause; whenever such a challenge comes from former supporters, it is particularly likely to be treated as anathema.

As a matter of fact, it was my initial articulation of disquiet about Kohut's treatment recommendations that led to the unpleasantness that compelled me to dissociate myself from Heinz's circle. To do him justice, Kohut himself never voiced any objection to my dissent; rather, he set about to rebut my point of view (see Kohut, 1977, chap. 1). In putting forth the claim that the appropriate end-point of the psychoanalytic treatment of disturbances involving the self – disorders he was later to define so as to include all psychopathology! – is the erection of compensatory mental structures, Kohut abandoned the psychoanalytic consensus that the proximate aim of treatment is to *know*, in favor of the ambition to effect a cure. Kohut was admirably clear about his radical departure from Freudian premises and values; in the last decade of his life he consistently repeated that he wished to replace insight with *empathy* as the primary goal of his therapeutic enterprise.

Obviously, such differences of opinion are both legitimate and commonplace. Similar disagreements about fundamental premises led to the ruptures between Freud and Adler (Stepansky, 1983) as well as between Freud and Jung (Gedo, 1983, chaps. 12–14). In such circumstances, neither protagonist is right or wrong: they are involved in disparate enterprises. In the present instance, the unanswered question is whether Kohut's enterprise can still be regarded as part of psychoanalysis, in view of his rejection of some of Freud's basic goals and values.

I feel very uneasy about assuming the mantle of Grand Inquisitor – after all, some sectarians might very easily claim that my own work is too unorthodox for their taste – and will therefore make no attempt to pronounce judgment on the psychoanalytic credentials of self psychology. Suffice it to say that there seems to be a degree of uncertainty on this very question, even among Kohut's heirs. On one hand, there are those who continue to see themselves as psychoanalysts and assert (as did Goldberg [1978] in his Introduction to *The Psychology of the Self*) that interpretation is the crucial curative factor in their work; on the other hand, many feel no allegiance to psychoanalysis and openly declare their adherence to a new therapeutic discipline (see Baker and Baker, 1987).

If self psychology is a novel professional discipline offering a new brand of psychotherapy, I have nothing to say about it, just as I have nothing to say about its countless competitors in the clinical marketplace. Judiciously conducted (see Basch, 1980) or administered with sufficient charisma, it is a system that is doubtless just as effective as most others. It is quite a different matter to perform psychoanalysis in accord with self-psychological assumptions, and that is the enterprise I propose to highlight in this chapter. Unfortunately, in actual practice, many clinicians obfuscate in this regard: for example, not long ago, as a guest instructor at a reputable psychoanalytic institute, I was presented a case report wherein the candidate/analyst (with the approval of his supervisor) decided on a therapeutic prescription of providing positively toned "mirroring," entirely on the basis of a brief history obtained in the initial consultation. I suspect that Kohut would have been horrified to learn of such attempts to misuse his ideas to adulterate psychoanalysis with the dross of a manipulated "corrective emotional experience." At least, I hope so.

From my vantage point, one of the primary virtues of self psychology is its freedom from the legacy of the metapsychology that organized psychoanalytic thinking for some 75 years. This advantage was not easily gained: when he embarked on his pioneering work, Kohut was the heir apparent of Heinz Hartmann, and through 1972 his writings were carefully cast in the mold of Hartmann's psychoeconomic postulates. It was only after Hartmann's death and Anna Freud's rejection of his proposed clinical innovations that Kohut was willing to listen to those of his friends – Michael Basch, Arnold Goldberg, and me – who had for years been urging him to abandon these untenable hypotheses. Clearly, many theoreticians who do not accept Kohut's point of view about clinical issues concur with his rejection of Freud's metapsychology (see Gill and Holzman, 1976); in American psycho-analysis, priority in this regard belongs to the students of David Rapaport.

For a few years, Kohut pursued his clinical investigations – which convinced him that drive theory was irrelevant to the issues he was attempting to conceptualize – without making a serious effort to think through the consequences of his findings for psychoanalytic theory as a whole. As a result of this choice of focus, he was content to use what he called two "complementary" theories (in analogy with the dual physical theories of light). This phase of his work was characterized by the distinction he made between "Tragic Man," unable to fulfill his own ambitions or to meet his ideals, and "Guilty Man," in conflict between his conscience and his appetites. In retrospect, this artificial dichotomy only divided the segment of the psychoanalytic field Kohut felt ready to view in terms of his own concepts from the residual issues he still saw within the framework of traditional clinical theories.

In his posthumous book, Kohut (1984) reversed himself on this score: he abandoned the self-indulgence of using two uncoordinated theoretical schemata simultaneously in favor of a unified self-psychological conceptualization, based on the notion of self–selfobject relations. Before commenting on the adequacy of this proposal as a replacement for Freud's drive theories as a unifying framework for psychoanalysis, I should state that some of his students preceded Kohut in concluding that a psychology of the self must be able to account for all the clinical phenomena encountered in the analytic situation. In particular, Terman (1976) showed that oedipal vicissitudes may be understood from the viewpoint of their impact on self-esteem and self-cohesion. My own earlier critiques of Kohut raised repeated objec-tions to the artificiality of the Tragic Man versus Guilty Man distinc-tion. I do not know, of course, whether Kohut bothered to read my publications after the estrangement between us, although I have very strong reasons to believe that my opinions continued to weigh heavily with him.

What did Kohut's ultimate psychological system, that of selfobject needs, selfobject functions, and self-selfobject relations, imply about human nature? Without being explicit, this conception of mental life regards bonding with a need-satisfying object as the sole norm of human existence, the only source of significant motives, and the only potential cause of maladaptation. Even if Kohut had broader criteria of selfobject functions than in fact he did, this view of mental life would seem exceedingly restrictive: as Stern (1985), among others, has concluded, much of human existence even during infancy presupposes solitude. But Kohut defined selfobject needs in an extraordinarily narrow manner; he confined them to those issues implicated in the regulation of self-esteem, namely, the idealization and subject-centered grandiosity he encountered in the consulting room (see Kohut, 1977, p. 33; 1978, p. 557).

However ubiquitous these human propensities may be, they do not adequately encompass even those contingencies evoked in the dyadic context of the psychoanalytic situation. At the very end of his life, Kohut (1984, pp. 193, 197, 203) began to realize that his classification of selfobject functions was incomplete. As a first step to remedy this deficiency, he proposed elevating so-called twinship transferences to the same conceptual plane hitherto occupied by idealizing and mirror transferences alone. What he failed to acknowledge was the probability that the need for an alter ego is much broader and more fundamental than the "narcissistic transferences" he had previously described (Kohut, 1968, 1971)–that the search for "twinship" is a consequence of lacunae in the patient's psychological skills, whereas idealization of others and the wish for affirmation are merely secondary effects of developmental difficulties of that kind (see Gedo, 1988).

Kohut's ultimate legacy to his followers is therefore likely to be this warning from the grave not to congeal his writings into self-psychological dogma, for in the backlash of the condemnation of his work for reductionism, the construction of a finished theoretical system threatens to obscure his valuable clinical discoveries. Arguments trying to prove that self psychology is less vulnerable on that score than are other reductionistic systems, such as that of Hartmann's ego psychology, are not likely to impress the coming generation of psychoanalysts, who will demand a clinical theory that accounts for the observations of every analytic faction.

From the clinical point of view, the greatest deficiency of Kohut's system is not its deemphasis of oedipal issues, as certain analytic traditionalists would have it; it is, in fact, perfectly feasible to deal with those conflicts through a self-psychological framework (see Terman,

1984/85). In my judgment, self psychology is weakest in its underemphasis on the effects of prior structuralization on the regulation of behavior. As a consequence, it promotes excessive optimism about the possibility of altering the personality by means of new (more empathic) experiences, without going to the trouble of painstakingly undoing existing pathogenic structures. Perhaps the most obvious example of this tendency is the neglect of patients' continuing hostile dispositions in favor of stressing that these were brought about by various noxious experiences suffered in childhood. But this selective inattention is by no means unique; Kohut has, in general, taken insufficient note of the unfavorable consequences for later adaptation of early identifications. That is how he blundered into the untenable position about the Oedipus complex that he adopted in his posthumous book: Kohut (1984) asserted that pathological outcomes of these developmental vicissitudes are invariably results of the parents' unempathic responses to the child's *current* behavior (pp. 6, 24, 68). Life is more complicated than that–in many instances, even in early childhood, it is the shadow of the past that has fallen upon the present.

A second major problem left unresolved by self psychology is an internal contradiction concerning the young child's reactions to failures on the part of caretakers to provide optimal life experiences. Kohut reached the conclusion that the resultant frustrations (and their psychopathological sequelae) are bound to be felt as injuries inflicted by the unempathic and disappointing "selfobjects" (see Kohut and Wolf, 1978, esp. p. 416; Kohut, 1978, p. 929). Indeed, on occasion Kohut went further, actually endorsing the accuracy of such an infantile view of the world by asserting (see Kohut, 1977, p. 29; 1984, p. 33) that caretakers may be expected to perform empathically enough to avoid the formation of psychopathology. At the same time, Kohut never repudiated his definition of "selfobject" as denoting a caretaker experienced as part of the subject's volitional system (Kohut, 1971, p. xiv). He often tried to illuminate this notion through the metaphor of a person's startled reaction to a paralyzed limb that no longer carries out his intentions. If this comparison of the reaction to a selfobject failure to a somatic catastrophe is apt, as I believe it is, it cannot at the same time be true that the victim of such a misfortune will attribute its causation to the caretaker/selfobject. He would, in fact, be more likely to experience it irrationally as a personal failure.

To be more precise, analysands may often try to blame their

psychopathology on the failures of their caretakers, but just as frequently they may assign the blame to themselves; and in many cases they are well aware that the crystalization of the personality is too complex a matter to be understood as having been formed by specific disappointments. In other words, patients' attitudes in adult life are not direct reflections of their initial childhood reactions to various crucial experiences, and those potentially pathogenic reactions cannot be eliminated from the mental life of analysands through empathy with childhood disappointments alone.

On paper, such exaggeration of the responsibility of caretakers for whatever goes wrong in early development may look like a relatively minor flaw in Kohut's system. I see it as a *major* problem because of its intimate connection with the role of empathy in Kohut's theory of treatment. Although he was at times explicit that empathy is merely a method of cognition (see Kohut, 1971, p. 300), in the main he avowed that the analyst should provide patients with "empathic acceptance" (Kohut, 1978, p. 899). Goldberg (1978) defined analytic empathy as "the proper feeling for and fitting together of the patient's needs and the analyst's response" (p. 8). Consequently, self psychology seems to expect that infantile attitudes of entitlement have to be validated by the analyst, that the analysand's persisting rage should be understood as the only appropriate response to the frustration of "selfobject needs," and that all misfortunes in early life could and should have been mastered through empathic parenting.

I have little doubt that a substantial number of patients may accept such authoritative verdicts, experience some diminution of guilt and shame, and even become less rageful as a result of such reassurance. Although this approach is often therapeutic, its beneficial results are obtained by means of a shared illusion, the echo of Rousseau's "noble savage" as the innocent babe. For even in those instances where childhood rage was provoked by parental failures (and, more emphatically, in all cases in which the childhood reaction was *not* caused by such errors), analysands can transcend these archaic transactions only if they grasp their inappropriateness in an adult context. And in the majority of cases children do not, in fact, end up disappointed with their caretakers; to the contrary, they tend to erect reaction formations against any disillusionment they may have suffered (see Gedo, 1975b).

Many self psychologists have espoused a view of therapeutic empathy that Kohut himself would certainly have rejected: in their mind empathy requires the application of Kohut's interpretive schema, as Schwaber (1987) has noted! To justify this ideological prejudice, they caricature alternative positions, usually by claiming that theories that are not self-psychological are experience distant, incapable of articulating the analysand's subjectivity, and can only lead to an outrageously frustrating therapeutic ambience. To be sure, these self-promoting attitudes seldom find their way into print, but I have encountered them with some frequency in personal discussions, and I have even heard them expressed in public meetings.

Although Kohut never indulged in such ideological terrorism, he was guilty of accusing those who would not accept his dictum that reliance on selfobjects is expectable throughout the life span of being unable to see the truth because of personal psychopathology (Kohut, 1984, p. 63). I wonder whether he would have admitted, in this ultimate period of his life and work, that his own viewpoint about the lifelong persistence of selfobject needs was a reflection of his own personal preferences? Earlier in his career, when I was on the best of terms with him, Kohut was proud to acknowledge that his insights about what he then called the narcissistic disorders had been gained through introspective, self-analytic work – in other words, that the selfobject needs he had discerned were his own. It is scientifically risky to build a clinical theory on putative understanding of one's own personality.

Kohut (1976) did not hesitate to point out that Freud's theory of neurosis was shaped by the latter's inner life, but he never seems to have realized that his own psychological horizons were equally bound to be circumscribed, that his brilliant introspective insights should not be turned into universals. Kohut (1968, 1971) discovered that excessive ambitions develop in early childhood as a result of various vicissitudes unconnected with parricide or incest, that failure to establish stable ideals is related to early disappointments with the caretakers, and that defects in self-esteem regulation are usually undergirded by tendencies to become disorganized or apathetic under stress. In my judgment, these were valid clinical observations that compelled Kohut's successors to reconsider the entire clinical theory of psychoanalysis. (For my version of such a reconsideration, see Gedo, 1979a.) Unfortunately, Kohut's own clinical theory focused too narrowly on issues previously understood under the rubric of "narcissism," presumably because these were the issues of paramount personal significance for him.

In conceiving of the psychological structure he called "the self" as bipolar, consisting of ambitions and ideals that must be fulfilled to achieve self-esteem, Kohut (1977, pp. 178, 243) reduced human motivations to the single issue of seeking perfection and deliberately chose to ignore biological, preverbal (and *a fortiori* presymbolic) influences on structuring the personality.[1] Kohut was slow to accept that his clinical findings demanded the postulation of a macrostructure formed before the secure differentiation of ego from id: as late as 1972, he still insisted that "self" refers only to a *content* of the mind (see Kohut, 1978, pp. 659–60). He acknowledged, in concluding *The Restoration of the Self,* that he had left unanswered the question of how self-as-structure is formed (see Kohut, 1977, p. 245). In the remaining years of his life, all he wrote on this score (Kohut, 1984, p. 70; Kohut and Wolf, 1978, p. 44) implied that it is the caretakers' empathic response to selfobject needs – that is, sufficient confirmation of the child's perfection and adequate maintenance of his view of their own – that determines self-formation.

Kohut's (1984) ultimate definition of "selfobject" (p. 52) was that of any entity that supports the cohesion, strength, and harmony of the self; in his view, the need for such supports is lifelong (Kohut, 1980a, p. 453; 1980b, p. 473). Kohut never addressed himself to two major questions: first, *why* conditions wherein the caretakers can be idealized, the child is affirmed in his expansiveness or provided with a silent double enhance the self-organization; second, how such experiences might lead to self-formation, understood as the development of specific sets of ambitions and ideals. Kohut's hypotheses about self-organization are too adultomorphic: they apply clinical findings about adult patients with defects in self-esteem regulation to the mental life of preverbal children. The issues Kohut discerned – which were originally termed "narcissistic transferences" – are properly referable to a phase of childhood wherein reflexive self-awareness already exists, a phase in which language is already available. Ironically, self psychology fails to address itself to the most fundamental issues of human existence, those biological matters that are built into the personality during infancy and form the core of "the self."

I can put this crucial point in still another way: Freudian psychoanalysis explored the intersystemic conflicts characteristic of the neu-

---

[1]It will be recalled that the range of biologically innate motivations is broad (see Hadley, 1989; Lichtenberg, 1989).

roses–the matters Kohut labeled the problems of "Guilty Man." Kohut's clinical observations led him to realize that a whole range of narcissistic issues–those he called the problems of "Tragic Man"–antedated and underlay neurotic conflicts. Instead of trying to correlate his new findings with the accumulated data of psychoanalytic experience (but see Gedo and Goldberg, 1973, esp. chap. 7), Kohut attempted to subsume all of mental life under the rubric of the vicissitudes of self-cohesion in various circumstances involving idealization/disillusionment and affirmation/lack of empathy. The inadequacy of this schema to explicate the totality of human mental life is most apparent from Kohut's failure to account for the frequent episodes of faulty tension-regulation he correctly observed: self psychology has had almost nothing to say about the disordered self!

To be sure, Kohut (1971) noted a wide variety of signs and symptoms of "fragmentation" or of emergency adaptive measures used to avert such disorganization, but he was not interested in the details of the regressive phenomenology or in their implications for the psychoanalytic theory of the mind. In parallel with this inattention to the antecedents of the cohesive self, in his statements about nosology, Kohut (1971, chap. 1) relegated to the category of psychoses conditions in which such self-cohesion has never been completely achieved–conditions about which he wrote nothing at all. It is true that Kohut (1984, p. 183) noted that so-called borderline patients are analyzable insofar as the analyst succeeds in organizing the bewildering phenomena presented by such analysands into some cognitive schema available to him–but Kohut never offered such a schema.

Kohut's pervasive tendency to ignore the work of most other contributors to psychoanalysis is nowhere more regrettable than in his failure to study the extensive literature on primitive personalities, where he could have learned about archaic mental states he seems not to have encountered in his analytic practice. (I have in mind clinical contingencies in the so-called borderline spectrum as described, for example, by such experienced therapists as Searles [1986].) Almost 20 years ago, in *Models of the Mind,* Arnold Goldberg and I (Gedo and Goldberg, 1973) postulated that such syndromes do not constitute disease entities but, rather, are expectable modes of functioning, acquired in the course of early development, evoked throughout the life span by specific adaptive requirements. These archaic response patterns are potentially available to everyone; in every analysis that goes far enough or deep enough such contingencies can be expected to arise. The best therapeutic results are obtained in those analyses which evoke transferences from every developmental level, including those preceding consolidation of a cohesive self; this is why I do not trust Kohut's (1977) recommendation that the analyses of disturbances affecting the self may appropriately be terminated when compensatory adaptive devices have been acquired. A personality built on quicksand is not likely to stand.

Ultimately, the least satisfactory aspect of self psychology may prove to be the extraordinarily reified notion of "self" in Kohut's writings. Not only does he anthropomorphize this construct in describing "the self" as a sentient being, capable of enfeeblement or vigor; what is more grave, in a literal acceptance of certain patients' concretization of their subjective state during these crises, he conceives of the regressive loss of self-cohesion as a fragmentation. The self is thereby reduced to a china figurine that, when smashed into bits, becomes a mass of dysfunctional shards. This notion is misleading, for neither analysands nor young children lose their functional capacities in a global way whenever they regress to a mode of organization that antedated self-cohesion.

Another way to state this objection to the reductionism of Kohut's view of human nature is to consider the inadequacy of his nosological system, particularly the one he promulgated after the creation of self psychology (see Kohut and Wolf, 1978). In this schema, the sole indicator of dysfunction is the patient's subjective state: is "the self" lacking in vigor, coherence, or harmony? Kohut postulated that empathic parenting (in his terms, adequate provision for selfobject needs) will succeed in creating a cohesive self, albeit maintenance of this state requires the continuing availability of selfobjects. If, as a result of selfobject failures, the infant does *not* develop a stable bipolar self, Kohut (1971, chap. 1) assumed that the resulting personality structure is either psychotic or barely compensated by means of avoidant–that is, schizoid–defenses designed to forestall injuries to self-esteem that would precipitate a psychotic decompensation.

In Kohut's schema, various forms of self disorder are accounted for by means of the concept of a "vertical split." As Basch (1967) was probably the first to point out, nonrepressive defenses such as disavowal are the mechanisms that maintain such mental conditions: splitting of the mind implies the simultaneous presence of mutually incompatible alternatives. Kohut was cognizant that a person's outward behavior may screen a broad spectrum of archaic mentation. On the other hand, he never acknowledged that in many instances we observe a primary failure to integrate the totality of personal aims into a cohesive self-organization, rather than the consequences of the defensively motivated splitting of a unitary hierarchy of aims (see Gedo and Goldberg, 1973, p. 99).

As I have tried to show in some detail elsewhere (Gedo, 1988), archaic pathology generally persists precisely because of a failure of integration of the relevant functions into the cohesive self, the aspect of mind that continues to mature with experience. In other words, the occurrence of islands of mulfunctioning, such as psychosomatic conditions, actual neuroses, or tics (to mention only a few of the more obvious types of archaic symptomatology in the presence of generally age-appropriate mental organization in adults), is best understood in terms of the frequent coexistence of separate subsets of "self nuclei" (Gedo and Goldberg, 1973, p. 65), one of which may undergo regression without involving the other in the process. Alternatively one self nucleus may remain arrested, giving rise to apraxias in otherwise adequate personalities. These are also the mental dispositions that permit the persistence of a "psychotic core" within an otherwise nonpsychotic personality, as Winnicott (1952) long ago noted. Complexities of this kind are left out of account in Kohut's work.

To recapitulate: Heinz Kohut deserves great credit for a decisive breakout from the restrictive paradigm of the transference neuroses. His work through 1972 lent clinical substance to the gathering movement to revise psychoanalytic theory (e.g., G. Klein, 1976; Schafer, 1976; Gill and Holzman, 1976; Rosenblatt and Thickstun, 1977; Gedo, 1979a), not only in the direction of abandoning the metapsychology based on Freud's physicalistic postulates but also by taking into account data from cases beyond the boundaries of the neuroses (see Gedo and Goldberg, 1973). Kohut's clinical material (see Kohut, 1971, 1977; Goldberg, 1978) dealt with issues more archaic than the infantile neuroses familiar to psychoanalysts. He convincingly demonstrated that some of these problems can be dealt with in psychoanalytic treatment conducted in the traditional manner if the transferences he defined as "narcissistic" are given due weight. Because these archaic mental dispositions are focused on the stability of the sense of self as well as issues of self-esteem, Kohut began to call his work "the analysis of the self."

This choice of psychoanalytic emphasis became transformed into the dissident school now named self psychology when analytic conservatives failed to accept Kohut's viewpoint. Probably in reaction to this polarization within the analytic community, Kohut attempted to formulate a clinical theory of universal applicability based on his new findings. This effort eventuated in a premature closure – a reductionistic theory, which, like its traditional predecessor, fails to take into account the legacy of all developmental phases and concentrates instead on derivatives of the specific nodal point in development that give rise to the adaptive difficulties found in the particular cases the study of which led to the formulation of the theory.

As I have pointed out for many years (see Panel, 1971), psychoanalytic clinical theory must integrate the data of our observations with children and adults of every type of personality organization; derivatives of different developmental phases need to be integrated in a hierarchical manner. The findings and concepts of Heinz Kohut should find their proper place within such a hierarchic view of self-organization. Alas, there are more things in heaven and on earth than are dealt with by self psychology.

CHAPTER 12

. —————————————— .

Psychoanalysis Transplanted to America

I t is ironic that psychoanalysis has perfused American culture to a far greater extent than it has that of any other community, for it is a characteristic product of that "Mittel-Europa" whose very existence remains generally unacknowledged in this country. It is widely known that Sigmund Freud, the creator of our peculiar discipline, profoundly mistrusted America and its potential influence on psychoanalysis, should his brainchild take root in the soil of a New World grounded in Puritan values. Naturally, Freud could not foresee that, as the 20th century progressed, American puritanism would be relegated to our cultural backwaters, to wage fatuous rear-guard actions about burning questions such as public funding for art with connotations that may shock Aunt Sally.

Despite the lame rationale for Freud's concern, however, we should keep in mind that the nature of the cultural surround has, all over the world, fundamentally altered psychoanalysis, giving rise to distinct national traditions, perhaps most clearly illustrated for Americans by the examples of France or Japan (see Turkle, 1978). The adherents of each of these intellectual currents almost always claim that they are simply the legitimate heirs of Freud – a natural, if myopic, attitude perhaps most prevalent in our immense country. I must say, in extenuation, that the mass flight of analysts from Central Europe two generations ago brought a majority of Freud's direct disciples to our shores and crippled the development of psychoanalysis in much of Europe for several decades. For some years after the second World War, psychoanalysis survived largely in American exile. We may therefore be pardoned for the parochialism that makes us unselfconscious about the ways in which our approach to the field has gradually departed from those of our colleagues abroad.

What are some of the significant features of contemporary psychoanalysis in America that lend our activities the distinctiveness of a regional dialect? One convenient way to answer this question is to focus on basic values that differentiate this community from most others. Strongest among these values is probably the *optimism* of a society ever seeking new frontiers. In scientific matters, such a philosophical position has lent unparalleled support to the search for new knowledge, support that includes financial backing for psychoanalytic investigators by private philanthropy as well as government agencies. Americans continue to show faith in the possibility of ameliorating almost any problem. Within the ranks of our profession, this optimism has produced both theoretical innovations and a prevalent therapeutic courage that stands in glaring contrast to Freud's conservatism about the possibilities of human change – witness the skeptical tone of his last statement on the subject, "Analysis Terminable and Interminable" (Freud, 1937).

One facet of American therapeutic ambitions has been the unceasing effort to broaden the scope of psychoanalysis-as-treatment to conditions previously thought to be unanalyzable – in Freud's classification, those beyond the boundaries of the transference neuroses. The psychanalytic hospital developed concurrently in this country and in Germany, but only here has it had an uninterrupted evolution, nourished, to be sure, by an infusion of European talent. But the astonishing success of psychoanalysis in infiltrating American psychiatry is by no means the sole manifestation of the therapeutic optimism we have displayed. It is equally manifest in the recurrent efforts to devise new forms of psychotherapy allegedly based on psychoanalytic premises but more certainly founded on the hope that, in circumstances that would defeat the application of psychoanalysis proper, the use of less rigorous techniques might succeed. In its most extreme form, this paradoxical attitude has led to claims for the superiority of "brief therapy" (Alexander, 1956; Gustafson, 1984); a more modest variant of such rosy views substitutes schedules of lesser frequency for Freud's analytic procedures. Until relatively recently, these manifestations of a "less is more" attitude were focused on cases deemed to be unanalyzable; I understand that such unreasoning optimism is now becoming fashionable even with respect to problems regarded to be most appropriately handled by means of analysis.

Beyond the realm of therapeutics, optimistic philosophies tend to underplay the role of unalterable, constitutional factors in pathogenesis, in favor of nurture psychologies that place greater stress on the influence of the environment. Consequently, we have witnessed the gradual deemphasis of the biological and neurological orientation Freud brought to the study of mind. This turn has meant, on one hand, a shift in the direction of theories centered on early object relations; the most Americanized of these variants are the "selfobject" concepts of self psychology that attribute any maladaptation to some failure on the part of the caretakers. On the other hand, the reluctance to accept the reality of constraints on human plasticity has led to a rejection of the significance of the repetition compulsion. This type of reductionism permits its proponents to dispense with the need for concepts linking the biological realm with that of subjectivity; in other words, they save themselves the trouble of articulating what Freud called "metapsychology." One segment of this group has seized upon a recent European intellectual import, that of hermeneutics, to buttress this characteristically American position.

There is, perhaps, slightly less agreement about the significance of the next quality of our psychoanalytic tradition that I wish to discuss, that of our prevailing *pragmatism*. In the form of a general disregard of such theoretical niceties as internal coherence, epistemological soundness, and other aspects of intellectual rigor, this focus on the practical and the instrumental turns its back on the greater part of Freud's agenda for psychoanalysis: his ambition to develop a science of mind and the possibility of making interdisciplinary contributions on the basis of such knowledge. "Yankee ingenuity" can rely on technical expertise alone. Within psychoanalysis, such anti-intellectualism is lent a veneer of respectability by claims that we can make do exclusively with so-called clinical theories, so that it is sufficient if our constructs are understood simply in a metaphorical sense. Pragmatists of this sort are unconcerned about conceptual clarity, provided they obtain therapeutic results that satisfy the customers. The increasing influence of such attitudes is sadly demonstrated by the marked diminution of psychoanalytic contributions in the interdisciplinary arena and the increasing reluctance of both journals and publishers to accept such works.

Some 25 years ago, Eissler (1958) attributed the pragmatic bent of American psychoanalysis to what he called "medical orthodoxy," that is, to the training of psychiatrist-analysts in the medical tradition, which has always given great weight to practical results. It has since become apparent that neither clinical psychology nor clinical social work produces candidates of a less pragmatic bent. In contrast to Freud, the Central European intellectual, American mental health professionals give priority to their vocation as healers, rather than committing themselves to a quest for knowledge. It was Rieff (1966) who first pointed out that Freudian psychoanalysis could be distinguished from other therapeutic systems, such as those of Jung and Adler, by its foreswearing the desire to cure. Twenty-five years ago, Rieff could already see the apostasy of American psychoanalysis in this regard. In the interval, this tendency has gathered strength, probably because of the gradual disappearance of European emigrés from the analytic community.

I do not mean to imply that in this respect (or, for that matter, in that of therapeutic hopefulness) the American position is necessarily disadvantageous. Although therapeutic ambition may provoke negativism, particularly on the part of analysands who may have felt exploited by their families for the latters' narcissistic gains, therapeutic indifference may be even more damaging, probably in a wider spectrum of cases. Persons who suffer from maladaptive characteristics hardly ever come for treatment because they wish to gain self-knowledge; they always desire to change (or at least to *be* changed) and require their analyst to be committed to that program. Analysts must not have private agendas, even curative ones, but if they cannot espouse their analysands' rational agendas to improve their adaptation, the results can be catastrophic. In this regard, American pragmatism is very helpful indeed and very much to be preferred to the attitude seemingly prevalent in France, for example, that regards psychoanalysis not as a treatment but as a species of intellectual exercise, akin to Freud's disastrous encounter with his patient "Dora" (Freud, 1905b). It is outrageous to disregard unfavorable therapeutic results because analysis has been completed in accord with process criteria. In other words, an absence of pragmatism would risk turning psychoanalysis into a vacuous sacred ritual.

I was very much struck, when I attended the 1982 Franco-American Psychoanalytic "Rencontre" in Paris, that most of the French participants regarded the American concern with adaptation (indeed, the entire legacy of Heinz Hartmann [1939, 1964] with regard to ego psychology) as a betrayal of the analysand's individuality in the interest of promoting submission to the requirements of society, often conceived of in Marxist terms as a bourgeois-capitalist society. Although such a view is clearly based on a misunderstanding (one that may not be devoid of some malice, at that), at the same time it should alert us to the pragmatic dangers of an excess of pragmatism. Our therapeutic zeal may save us from conducting empty analytic rituals, but it may covertly lead us into permitting our activities to degenerate into behavioral training, analogous to the amazing feats of certain circus performers with wild animals.

Let me now turn to the characteristic I consider to be the most significant among those I have selected for discussion, the adherence of American psychoanalysis to *empiricism*. This is, of course, an adherence typical of our intellectual life as a whole, of our legacy as inheritors of the British philosophical tradition of the 17th and 18th centuries. You will recall that it was this philosophical position that made possible the great flowering of science in the age of Enlightenment. Insofar as we are empiricists, we view psychoanalysis as a science of mental functions—an attitude many colleagues in other countries do not share with us. Freud, who has rightly been called a Biologist of the Mind (Sulloway, 1979) was also an empiricist, in part, but his philosophical position was a more complex one that balanced this empiricism with a strong admixture of *rationalism*—more of which later.

The willingness of American psychoanalysis to submit to tests of empirical validation was clearly demonstrated a generation ago through its participation in (and response to) epistemological discussions of its scientific status (Hook, 1959), a process recently repeated in the dialogue between members of our discipline and the philosopher Adolf Grünbaum (1984; see also Edelson, 1984). A substantial portion of the American psychoanalytic literature is devoted to empirical studies of various kinds: follow-ups, outcome studies, studies of analytic process, validation studies focused on specific hypotheses, and the like. The recent upsurge of enthusiasm about psychoanalytic infant research is only the climax of a movement to test our developmental propositions by means of the direct observation of children that started 40 years ago with the pioneering projects led by Ernst Kris in New Haven, René Spitz in Denver, and Margaret Mahler in New York. It is not my intention to survey the gamut of empirical research in psychoanalysis performed in this country; suffice it to say that nothing like it has taken place anywhere else in the world.

The great virtue of psychoanalytic empiricism is its conservative influence in preventing the espousal of unwarranted conclusions. To be sure, such a safeguard against charlatanism tends to be applied in a double standard: quite strictly with regard to new hypotheses but in desultory fashion about the conventional wisdom. In this sense, American psychoanalysis has been more resistant to change than have its counterparts abroad. At the same time, it is blessedly free of extremist factions. Our standards of discourse are unusually civilized because we tend to adhere to the accepted ground rules of science as a whole. In case you are tempted to take such blessings for granted, just recall the corrosive effects of ideologically based disputation about scientific matters, such as the Stalinist attacks on psychoanalysis as a reactionary doctrine. I have personally experienced Marxist heckling while presenting papers at certain Italian universities, and I can attest to the difference between such confrontations and the fertile intellectual challenge of scientific discourse.

At the same time, our commitment to empiricism has led to some overvaluation of research methods that rely on positivist criteria of validation, especially in comparison with an exchange of scientific ideas whose persuasiveness lies in internal coherence, economy of means, or congruence with the reader's personal and clinical experiences. This overvaluation indicates we tend to fall into scientism, the inappropriate imitation of experimental science in fields of investigation that do not lend themselves to the manipulation of a small number of variables. *Pari passu* we generally neglect the potentialities of our own therapeutic work as a source of clinical conclusions, particularly if they are pooled with data that can be provided by colleagues. The scientific method calls for the replication of every investigative effort: errors or illusory data are just as likely to be reported in quantitative studies as in the narrative account of a single case. Such case studies are very much a part of empirical science, but the assessment of their significance belongs to another epistemic domain, that of rationalism.

A few years ago, an English translation of Rapaport's (1974) dissertation concerning the history of philosophical psychology was finally published. Rapaport there pointed out that Freud's methodology followed the tradition of Immanuel Kant, who had attempted to reconcile empiricism and rationalism, positions that crystalized as opposing viewpoints at the beginning of the 17th century, under the influence of Descartes. You will recall that Freud made use of features that characterize a rationalist epistemology beyond mere deductive reasoning–among these, he often postulated the presence of innate ideas, such as the occurrence of universal symbols. This aspect of rationalism is unacceptable from an empiricist vantage point; many Freudian ideas, such as the death instinct, have been rejected in America because they are utterly lacking in empirical referents. I do not bring this matter up in order to take any personal position in these age-old controversies, but only to underscore the judgment that American psychoanalysis has the very unusual characteristic of making little or no use of rationalism.

Our refusal to listen to the siren song of reason does safeguard us against arbitrary notions that seem plausible simply because they are logical. Thus, the concept of psychic energy was discredited in America as soon as its lack of empirical underpinnings became clear (see G. Klein, 1976). Incidentally, aside from the absurdist efforts to claim that it is scientifically tenable to retain this concept as a metaphor for a subjective state, the only serious defense of Freud's idea I know of is Opatow's (1989), an essay wherein the source of the concept is traced to Hegel and its philosophical legitimacy is effectively defended. Naturally, most of us remain unconvinced: 19th-century philosophers knew nothing about the functioning of the nervous system!

Conversely, our contempt for mere "speculation" may also cost us dearly. Our journals and symposia pay scant attention to the internal logic of the papers they present; critiques of theoretical proposals on rationalist grounds (such as Benjamin Rubinstein's devastating rebuttal of the advocates of purely "clinical" theories [for the argument as a whole, see Gill and Holzman, 1976]) have scarcely found an audience among us. My own critique of certain theoreticians on the ground that their work is incoherent (Gedo, 1986) was found shocking by one reviewer (H. Friedman, 1988), who regards those authors as highly eminent and admirable because they have influenced so many of our colleagues. It is true that this rejection of my rationalist argument was more pragmatic than empirical. At the same time, it illustrates the last characteristic of psychoanalysis in America that I wish to discuss here: its adherence to our shared civic religion. In the jargon of philosophy, this attitude would probably be classified as a manifestation of *irrationalism*.

It seems paradoxical that a community devoted to empiricism should, at the same time, be characterized as one committed to a set of irrational beliefs. Yet we are quite familiar with the human propensity for inconsistency as a consequence of splitting the mind through disavowals. As Thomas Aquinas put it, we have *beliefs* precisely because we regard them as absurd. In other words, faith supervenes in matters not subject to empirical validation. Thus, our civic values can be espoused with religious fervor without overtly threatening our scientific credentials. There may be practical limits to the latitude we allow ourselves in these matters, but they are quite broad. In other countries, at any rate, less fortunate psychoanalysts have been unable to adhere to our profession while they were forced to espouse tyrannies of the Left or the Right.

Many of the values shared by Americans are generally characteristic of the Western world in the modern era. Most prominently, the commitment of psychoanalysis to freedom and dignity is also the foundation of the liberal consensus of Europe and North America since the mid-18th century. Some features of American civic religion are, however, by no means prevalent in many places where psychoanalysis has flourished; least of all was it so in the Habsburg Empire in Freud's lifetime. To return to the example of my recent transgression against one of these shibboleths, I suspect that I aroused the reviewer's ire because he experienced my rationalism as unabashedly elitist. What could I say? "Kantians of the World, unite; you have nothing to lose but your Reason"?

The elitism of experience, reason, and knowledge, the qualities that constitute the stock-in-trade of an effective psychoanalytic clinician, is in fact not compatible with the egalitarianism of American society. This dysjunction threatens to impair even our capacity to illuminate our analysands' "ego defects," lest we appear to inflate ourselves at their expense in some oracular manner. Even if we do manage to maintain our "expertise" in our consulting rooms, however, our collective need to remain "just regular folks" has a deleterious effect on our intellectual standards. It is becoming less and less feasible to disqualify applicants, candidates, or aspirants for faculty positions or training analyst appointment on the ground of their failure to meet some qualitative standard. Raising the question of talent has become an un-American *faux pas*. Very recently, another reviewer (Collins, 1990) expressed astonishment that, in a book on creativity (Gedo, 1983), I still espouse the old-fashioned concept of "genius"!

Another article of faith in America is the relevance of the concept of fairness to human affairs in general. In most other communities, this value is applied only in the context of games, as the principle of "fair play." Our sense of justice has gradually tilted in the direction of requiring what we refer to as a "level playing field" that will eliminate competitive disadvantages. Needless to say, this unwillingness to accept the luck of the draw impels us to attempt various measures intended to restore fair conditions even in circumstances that do not promise adequate returns – witness some of the extraordinary efforts to compensate the handicapped by means of staggering expenditures that can do nothing to eliminate their disadvantages. I do not raise this issue as a matter of public policy; I want to confine my discussion to its relevance for our functioning as psychoanalysts.

In large measure this sense of universal entitlement to an affectively gratifying existence has constrained many among us to jettison the Freudian prescription for an analytic attitude of equidistance (sometimes called "neutrality") with regard to various aspects of intrapsychic conflicts. In certain quarters, this bias in favor of narcissistic gratification has gone so far as to recommend that we refrain from trying to ascertain the truth if such an effort threatens to cause our patients some mortification (see Kohut, 1973). The American ethos demands that psychological treatment compensate our less than fortunate fellow men who need our assistance by providing them with an "empathic" ambiance (Wolf, 1976), as if what ailed them were a deficiency disease we could overcome by supplying affirmative human experiences (see Pine, 1989). By contrast, the usual psychoanalytic view is that what is done is done and cannot be undone: traumata can be mastered only by reexperiencing their bitterness.

Instead of listing more examples of the effects of local conditions and attitudes on American psychoanalysis, I should now like to turn to a consideration of the cumulative effects of such national characteristics on an enterprise created within the subjective matrix of one person's mental universe 100 years ago. Freud was closer to philosophical pessimism than to optimism, if not as despairing on that score as his great countryman and near-contemporary, Franz Kafka. He was committed to the search for knowledge, albeit he made pragmatic concessions to gain a public hearing, unlike his immediate predecessor, Friedrich Nietzsche. Freud followed Kant's way, not the simpler empiricism of Hume and Locke or the rationalism of Descartes, thus differentiating himself from Ernst Mach and Ludwig Wittgenstein. He was an aristocrat of the spirit, who preached that man must submit to necessity (*Ananke*), and a skeptic about notions of egalitarianism or fairness. In this regard, he had no peer in Central Europe or, for that matter, few anywhere else. Is it possible to carry on his legacy in the America of the 1990s?

Obviously, we must allow a hundred psychoanalytic flowers to bloom, and none needs to be identical to its historical antecedents; after all, the general public has insisted on calling even Jungian therapy "psychoanalysis," although Jung himself did his best to give it another designation. But we would do well to devise a rational taxonomy of post-Freudian developments in psychoanalysis, so-called. As I have tried to show, most of the American varieties betray common characteristics that Freud would very likely have found highly distasteful. I do not mean that we must therefore accept the contemptuous judgments of certain chauvinists who belong to other traditions—Freud would, in all likelihood, have found their versions of psychoanalysis just as unpalatable as ours. It is, however, dangerous to believe that the versions that thrive in "God's country" have profited from Divine Inspiration.

The other side of the coin is that we have no reason ever to be embarrassed about the American versions of psychoanalysis. There is nothing whatsoever wrong with hopefulness, practicality, scientific skepticism, or commitments to fairness, equality, individualism, and personal liberty. Every conceivable philosophical and ethical position has pitfalls of the kind I have tried to outline in our own case. Viewed from the shores of Lake Michigan, the dangers of French or Japanese habits of mind seem much greater than do the disadvantages of our own. Moreover, we are usually more inclined to import ideas from abroad than are our colleagues in other communities, so that our eccentricities are more likely to be mitigated by outside influences than are those of most others.

Finally, it also needs to be stated that the Central European culture so brilliantly represented by Sigmund Freud no longer exists. It could not survive a disastrous half century of Nazism and Communism; Mittel-Europa is prostrate and, when it recovers, it is unlikely to do so in a form deriving from its early 20th-century past. That past has survived only in exile, largely in America, changed for better and for worse by its transplantation into a new world.

CHAPTER 13

• ———————————————— •

Ilion Besieged
A Tenth-Year Report

We are on the threshold of being able to commemorate the centenary of our origins as a discipline, Freud's initial psychotherapeutic efforts as a private practitioner. I have been deeply immersed in psychoanalysis, as a student and as a practitioner, for some 40 years and was primed to enter the profession (in part through family connections in Budapest and Prague) well before starting medical school. I begin on this personal note in order to clarify the subjective bias that colors my view of the last 10 years of psychoanalytic history: I have lived within psychoanalysis longer than I have dwelt in America – I might even claim that it is the only community in which I do not feel like an exile. Family myth has it that in old age my paternal grandfather overcame his bronchial asthma by reading Freud. When? About seven decades ago. In an expansive mood, I have been heard to say, "La psychoanalyse, c'est moi!" When I am seized with bitterness about the politics of our undisciplined discipline, I curse it as a *cosa nostra*.

The person who had the greatest impact on me as a teacher was my countrywoman, Therese Benedek, whose brief analysis with Ferenczi took place before 1920. When she was close to 80, I had the wit to ask Therese to comment on her 60 years of professional experience in psychoanalysis, especially on the increasing amounts of time apparently needed to accomplish the therapeutic task. Amused by the naive scientism implicit in my inquiry, she replied that the effects of analytic insights were farther reaching when these revelations about the human condition were still new! Perhaps the legend about my grandfather Miksa's introspective feats is not so unbelievable, after all. Keys to the secrets of nature probably work best when they are possessed by relatively few. The pioneers of psychoanalysis have been described as a band of marginal cultists, and not without justification. It is equally cogent, however, to recognize that they felt themselves to be an elite in possession of a powerful, if esoteric, truth. A German film of the 1920s, for which Karl Abraham served as a consultant, called its psychoanalyst/hero *Der Seelensucher*–an explorer of the soul. Where, nowadays, are the snows of yesteryear?

In the aftermath of the second world war, the analytic community, centered almost exclusively in the United States and Britain, was still small enough for most of its members to get to know each other. That was the exclusive company my generation of candidates aspired to join. Those of us who ultimately qualified began to make our presence felt in analytic organizations and by way of publications through the 1960s; we joined the faculties of analytic institutes five or ten years later and were ready to step into positions of leadership around 1980. By that time, however, the explosive growth of psychoanalysis beyond the boundaries of the English-speaking world, with the concomitant growth of the International Psycho-Analytic Association, had rendered obsolete our sense that we had been anointed through some quasi-apostolic succession. Competing cliques had seized the major channels of psychoanalytic communication, which they proceeded to bend to their partisan purposes, and various Pied Piers tried to attract our young with tunes calculated to win popular favor. In this chaotic environment, very few islands of reasonable and ecumenical discourse emerged.

Everyone – well, almost everyone! – seems to look back on the past decade as a succession of disasters for American psychoanalysis. (Those who are aware that some of our colleagues overseas are thriving seem convinced that *their* inevitable time of troubles is fast approaching.) We have lost popular favor, scientific prestige, insurance coverage, tax deductibility, influence within psychiatric training centers. We are even worse off than the French king, Francis I, after his disaster at

Pavia: he was able to write his mother, from captivity, "All is lost, but my honor." I am not certain that we have been able to keep ours. Contrary to our professed principles, we have failed to look inward for explanations of our ongoing collapse. We have diligently externalized the blame onto governments unconcerned with the public welfare, sensationalist news media intolerant of complexity, rival mental health professionals willing to underbid us, a decadent society that produces few analyzable neurotics, and a younger cohort of potential candidates unwilling to make the financial sacrifices necessary to pursue our calling. Our defenses are professionally skillful: the charges we make are accurate enough, but we fail to acknowledge that the conditions we decry need not have damaged our profession if it were otherwise sound, for they are fundamentally extrinsic to our appropriate functions.

The crux of our profession's vulnerability to the unfavorable social milieu is our unverbalized insistence on two mutually exclusive goals: on one hand, on continually increasing our numbers; on the other, on continuing to participate in the uninterrupted, progressive enrichment of the American upper bourgeoisie. As expectable demands for analytic services gradually saturated more and more metropolitan areas, the only ways for analysts to keep pace with the earning power of other professionals (not to speak of business or of the entertainment world) were either to devote increasing amounts of time to nonanalytic work (even to activities beyond the realm of patient care) or to broaden our criteria of analyzability and thus expand our clientele.

I believe that the decisive change within psychoanalysis to take place in the past decade has been the silent abandonment of caution about the ambition to analyze almost anyone willing to try what we have to offer. At the same time, reluctance to recommend psychoanalysis to prospective patients has led to a putative shortage of that endangered species and, *pari passu*, to the vast expansion of opportunities to keep such people in (lucrative) therapies of various sorts, although these treatments offer no reasonable hope of ameliorating their problems. (Under the circumstances, the pharmacological methods of our psychiatric colleagues commend themselves as simpler, cheaper, and less tainted by commercialism.) At any rate, the contemporary analytic scene reveals thousands of therapists who have had analytic training, do little or no psychoanalysis, but exercise a decisive voice in the councils of our professional organizations. At the same time, those of us who are committed to the analytic method (at the very least, to the use of free association and to sessions at the maximum frequency our schedule permits) tend to occupy ourselves with analyses of unprecedented difficulty.

Neither of these strategies has salutary consequences: the retreat from analysis transforms the individual practitioner's adherence to our ranks into an empty political slogan and tends to turn our organizations into trade associations (which may even be accused at times of restraint of trade!). For its part, the option to plunge ahead despite all obstacles has produced less than happy therapeutic results, as a growing number of follow-up studies cited elsewhere in this book have clearly shown. Parenthetically, those of our colleagues who perform few analyses probably do no better, when they do try, than do the overambitious, for clinical skills must be honed through continual practice. All in all, then, our discipline can seldom claim impressive successes and has therefore fallen into disrepute with an increasingly cynical public. Hence, efforts to reverse our loss of external support seem doomed: only a policy of radical retrenchment and great improvement in the therapeutic skills of our membership could halt the vicious circle I have described.

Unfortunately, neither of these desirable goals is likely to be achieved in the foreseeable future. There is simply no way of restricting entry into the profession, for whatever criteria we might use to do so will be outflanked by the creation of rival training programs willing to waive those specific requirements – witness the recent spread of new institutes under the aegis of Division 39 of the American Psychological Association. (We shall be fortunate, in fact, if we can avoid the deprofessionalization of psychoanalysis through the setting up of training for mere technicians.) Moreover, most analysts seem to be happier when their discipline is expanding its numbers, and psychoanalytic educators are panicked at the thought of not having anyone to teach. (We cannot forget that analytic candidates are an important source of business for those who are designated as Training Analysts.)

The production of more effective analysts is impossible to manage precisely because the discouraging results of our traditional procedures have led to the rupture of our former consensus about the theory of technique, a condition that has secondarily led to an inability to agree on what constitutes analytic competence. The rancorous controversy about the contributions of Heinz Kohut that has characterized the past decade is only the most prominent of these impossible-to-negotiate discords. Some years ago, I devoted an entire book, *Conceptual Issues in Psychoanalysis* (Gedo, 1986), to the dynamics of such fissures of our professional community, and I will not repeat that thesis here. Suffice it to say that they generally lead to the adoption of reductionist attitudes, espousing one cogent but partial truth at the expense of others and denigrating the views of competing theoreticians. In our training organizations and certifying bodies, we have imposed an uneasy truce that permits the rival camps to have the credentials of their potential adherents approved. Besides – the more the merrier!

As I see the history of the 1980s, then, this was the time when collectively we finished painting ourselves into a nasty corner. Buttressed by the residual transferences of the younger generation of analysts, those of us in positions of authority and leadership have persevered in the status quo, without even admitting, as did Louis XV, that our inertia would unleash a deluge upon our successors. To put this in a manner more congruent with the spirit of our time, we did not confess that we felt, "I've got *mine*, Jack!" Nor did we give any thought to whether or not what we have is worth holding.

The issue I have just touched on permits me to describe in still another way the decisive changes that took place in our community in the past decade. In the course of the 1980s, membership in that community ceased giving the majority among us much support or satisfaction. Probably as a consequence of the fact that most analysts experience few successes in performing clinical psychoanalyses, hitherto unprecedented pressures have developed to fulfill other ambitions within the profession. One aspect of this self-promoting tendency has been the desire to use our qualifications to earn as much money as possible. Not only has this attitude led to pricing much of our natural constituency (academics, students, creative artists, nurses, social workers, government officials, etc.) out of the market; what is equally serious is the general acceptance of the propriety of retaining any patient for one's own practice. Instead of referring potential analysands to our low-fee clinics (or to the occasional colleague who prefers gaining analytic experience to maximizing income), most people nowadays offer these patients some brand of psychotherapy. It is also extremely rare now, in contrast to the days of my apprenticeship, for analysts to decide that a particular analysand might be better served by working with someone else.

I do not mean to suggest that financial prosperity is an unworthy goal (or that I have taken a vow of poverty), but we have to some degree succumbed to its potentially corrupting influence. Perhaps I can best make my point by retelling my favorite analytic anecdote for the 1980s. Some years ago, the local institute invited a distinguished humanist scholar to give a public lecture under its auspices. Upon his arrival in town, one of the trustees gave a reception in his honor in her elegant apartment in one of the most prestigious buildings of the city. Very few psychoanalysts were present; I happened to be invited only because my wife had a personal relationship with the lecturer. Our hostess had a superb art collection; scarcely knowing anyone there, I was wandering from picture to picture, sipping the champagne appropriate for the occasion. I was awakened from my reverie when I bumped into the trustee's analyst, who was surveying the scene from the vantage point of a window overlooking one of America's most impressive townscapes. Affectionately, my colleague put an arm around my shoulders and whispered, "John, *this* is psychoanalysis!" And there is no way of chasing such money-changers from our Temple.

Beyond the financial arena, the most popular venue for unleashing our ambitions has been the organizational one. Everyone must acquire a title; we are an army of staff officers without troops. Democratic slogans have been used to screen the establishment of bloated bureaucracies: everyone has to be involved in governance. Our organizations are complex enough to rule medium-sized banana republics. The faculties of many institutes outnumber their student bodies. It would all be quite amusing, like some turn-of-the-century Viennese operetta, except that this politicization of bodies that have scientific and educational functions has severely impaired the standards everyone has piously promised to uphold. Witness the current hue and cry about granting all graduates of its institutes automatic full membership in the American Psychoanalytic Association: if successful, this ingathering of flocks will instantaneously add hundreds to its roster, including a large number with glaring deficiencies in training or who are the beneficiaries of "compassionate graduation" from institutes well aware of these candidates' lack of competence but eager to keep their institutions busy – and profitable for the faculties.

Of course, there are perfectly good reasons to keep a professional membership organization open to almost anyone willing to pay its dues, but such trade associations are not allowed to influence either the education of candidates for the profession or its certification process. Unfortunately, we might gain almost nothing by insulating our schools from the populist pressures of nonacademic practitioners, for large numbers of our educators espouse the very same attitudes. As the director of one large institute told me recently, when I complained about our policy of training as many analysts as possible, regardless of need for their services, "Our people [i.e., the faculty] want work." When I reminded him that such a policy on the part of a professional school smacks of commercial fraud, he asked to switch our friendly conversation to a more pleasant topic.

I realize, of course, that my adoption of the tone of Jeremiah, thundering against the sins of his people, is both unpleasant and liable to be dismissed as objectionably elitist. I am, in fact, in favor of democratic governance. One of these days I would like to write a Jeremiad against the tyranny of small oligarchies in some of our institutions; but that topic is not specifically relevant for the history of the 1980s, for it has bedeviled us ever since Freud formed a secret inner circle to put down the analytic peasants. I do not believe it is elitism to graduate only analysts who do competent analytic work, to certify only those who are able to demonstrate their competence by means of written reports, to appoint to our faculties only those who have mastered our literature and have the skill to communicate what they know to an audience of students. Although these desiderata are often given lip service, they are even more often honored in the breach. My contention is best illustrated by the outraged reaction from many institutes when the recently constituted Committee on Non-Medical Clinical Training of the American Psychoanalytic Association fails to approve a substantial portion of applicants they would like to recruit. They scream, "Kill the umpire!" pretending that the application of a (none too high) standard of eligibility is not being fairly administered. In point of fact, although minor inequities are inevitable because of shifting committee personnel, my many years of experience on this and other review committees have convinced me that they are conscientious to a fault. It is precisely because one has no conflict of interest in judging the credentials of applicants to other institutes that national committees can be appropriately selective—local institutes hardly ever are.

At any rate, the past decade has marked the disappearance of any pretense on the part of organized psychoanalysis to being a discipline of scholars, scientists, humanists, or even educated people. Perhaps such fantasies were never part of the American scene—Freud himself was greatly apprehensive about the possible Americanization of his brainchild—and they remained tenable only as long as colleagues transplanted from Europe possessed a disproportionate share of influence in our community. That generation is no longer contributing in significant ways. I suspect that I may now be one of the most experienced European-born analysts who is still active in this country, and I was barely adolescent when I was transplanted here. Let us recall that the influx of *trained* analysts, as well as the process of Americans seeking acculturation in the Old World, came to a permanent halt a full 50 years ago. And it is not mere antinativist snobbism on my part to note that our younger colleagues scarcely participate in the cultural life of our communities or that hardly any of us ever read serious literature.

As I mentioned in the previous chapter, Eissler (1958) attributed the early manifestations of these phenomena to the "medical orthodoxy" of psychoanalysis in America. Today we would have to translate this into an orthodoxy encompassing all the mental health professions—that of a narrow specialization as healers. No wonder that the membership of the American Psychoanalytic Association voted, on the question of extending recruitment beyond psychiatrists, to accept persons with master's degrees in social work or psychiatric nursing. There is certainly nothing wrong with experienced practitioners in these disciplines as healers—but what a comedown from aspirations to be *Seelensuchern!* The more we lapse into acceptance of a role as mere therapists—with a corresponding diminution in our collective capacity to uphold the humanist portion of the Freudian program—the more impoverished psychoanalysis will become even in the therapeutic arena, for our analytic effectiveness does not as yet depend on the precise application of some psychotechnology; it is largely a measure of what we *are*, not what we intentionally *do* in our consulting rooms.

Even if we choose to disregard the therapeutic and intellectual disadvantages of this gradual shift in the direction of a technical discipline, it is important to note that it constitutes a difficult-to-reverse alteration in the very nature of the analytic enterprise. I believe it is the principal factor in the ever-increasing clamor by candidates and recently graduated analysts for instruction in how to deal with various contingencies in treatment. Would it have been conceivable, even a decade ago, to entitle an analytic monograph "Six Steps in the Treatment of" some putative nosological entity? Yet that is the designation of a successful work of today by an eminent contributor to our field.

The reverse of the same coin is the general lack of comprehension that seems to greet contributions that do not deal directly with concrete issues. Not long ago, I had the privilege of introducing the plenary speaker at the spring meeting of the American Psychoanalytic Association. Disquieted by the frequent dismissals of his previous presentations as mere poetry, he requested that I inform the audience of the actual purport of his work. I therefore tried to spell out that his was a consistent effort to discern the epistemological consequences of the limitations of the human capacity to classify information. Soon after this event, I received a letter of thanks from the speaker, who wrote that my efforts were quite successful: his spies reported overhearing, on the way out of the hall, comments that the paper was "just philosophy–you know, like the lectures we heard in college." Indeed.

It is somewhat ironic that this turn in the direction of simple-minded pragmatism should have occurred at a time marked by a decided resurgence in the interest of scholars in other disciplines in what psychoanalysis might be able to contribute to their scholarly armamentaria. This ferment has been most notable in the fields of literature and biography, but it has also affected certain branches of history, creativity studies, and the history of art; scarcely any field within the humanities has escaped it altogether. At the same time, publications of these promising interdisciplinary endeavors do not seem to interest psychoanalysts, if the complaints of publishers are to be believed. I happen to believe them, for I have followed developments in some of these subfields rather closely, and the number of active participants from within psychoanalysis in each of these endeavors is pitifully small.

Of course, our publishers also complain about matters they consider more serious than the decline in the marketability of high culture. The economics of the book trade have forced consumers to buy more selectively, and the proliferation of competing publishers (as well as authors) has made it very difficult to ensure success for most books. Actually, "success" has probably always meant sales to a broader public than the psychoanalytic community, so that the significance of such distribution is in fact quite ambiguous. Nonetheless, one gets the overall impression that psychoanalysts generally no longer try to keep up with the current literature, as many tried to do in the past. Perhaps this is merely a manifestation of the general decline of the print media, but I suspect that it may be a more specific by-product of our increasing preoccupation with therapeutic skills. After all, these cannot very well be acquired through reading. Theoretical issues no longer seem to excite most psychoanalysts; books about these matters do even less well than others, and very few of them have appeared in the past decade.

One fascinating consequence of these manifold changes of focus is that clinical proposals are seldom judged on the basis of internal coherence or congruence with other aspects of unchallenged psychoanalytic tenets. (Well, why not consider them in isolation, in a culture devoted to unreason, in an age when we can choose presidents because they say the right things about the Pledge of Allegiance or prison furloughs?) In such a climate, extremist positions, put forward in a polemical spirit, tend to find greater favor than do more carefully stated, nonreductionist, ecumenical propositions. Was it Anatole France who claimed that the majority is always wrong?

As I review what I have written, I am reminded of the Marschallin's autumnal soliloquy in *Der Rosenkavalier.* Perhaps I have simply confessed that, suddenly, I have become superannuated. (Or, worse, I am Verdi's "vecchio John," Falstaff!) In one's seventh decade, one is both entitled and expected to grumble about the inadequacies of the younger generation. Yet, even if we leave open the question of the ultimate significance of the changes I deplore, there can be no doubt about the conclusion that the psychoanalytic world I aspired to join over 40 years ago is entirely dead. Many other aspects of the world that mattered to me have also disappeared, but some have triumphantly survived adversity – witness the current return of Central Europe into the orbit of Western civilization, to the values of my grandfathers. And I am not an opponent of innovation – least of all within psychoanalysis itself. After all, scarcely anyone has published as radical a set of psychoanalytic ideas in the past decade as have I. Like Cassandra, I am ever hopeful that my pessimistic prophecies might still be heard, that I might stimulate my colleagues to join me in promoting a viable course for our discipline as an intellectual endeavor of the highest order.

REFERENCES

Abraham, K. (1924), A short study of the development of the libido viewed in the light of mental disorders. In: *Selected Papers on Psycho-Analysis*. London: Hogarth Press, 1942, pp. 418–49.

Alexander, F. (1956), *Psychoanalysis and Psychotherapy*. New York: Norton.

_____ & French, T. (1946), *Psychoanalytic Therapy*. New York: Ronald Press.

Arlow, J. & Brenner, C. (1964), *Psychoanalytic Concepts and the Structural Theory*. New York: International Universities Press.

Baker, M. & Baker, H. (1987), Heinz Kohut's self psychology. *Amer. J. Psychiatry*, 144:1–9.

Basch, M. (1967), On disavowal. Presented at the Institute for Psychoanalysis, Chicago.

_____ (1975a), Perception, consciousness, and Freud's "Project." *The Annual of Psychoanalysis*, 3:3–19. New York: International Universities Press.

_____ (1975b), Psychic determinism and freedom of will. Presented at the Institute for Psychoanalysis, Chicago.

_____ (1975c), Toward a theory that encompasses depression: A revision of existing causal hypotheses in psychoanalysis. In: *Depression and Human Existence*, ed. E. Anthony & T. Benedek. Boston: Little, Brown, pp. 483–534.

_____ (1976a), The concept of affect: A re-examination. *J. Amer. Psychoanal. Assn.*, 24:759–777.

_____ (1976b), Psychoanalysis and communication science. *The Annual of Psychoanalysis*, 4:385–422. New York: International Universities Press.

_____ (1976c), Theory formation in Chapter VII: A critique. *J. Amer. Psychoanal. Assn.,* 24: 61–100.

_____ (1980), *Doing Psychotherapy.* New York: Basic Books.

_____ (1983), The perception of reality and the disavowal of meaning. *The Annual of Psychoanalysis,* 11:125–154. New York: International Universities Press.

Breuer, J. & Freud, S. (1895), Studies on hysteria. *Standard Edition,* 2. London: Hogarth Press, 1955.

Bridger, W. (1989), Presidential address. Presented to the Society for Biological Psychiatry.

Calef, V. & Weinshel, E. (1981), Some clinical consequences of introjection: Gaslighting. *Psychoanal. Quart.,* 50:44–66.

Collins, B. (1990), Review of John E. Gedo's *Portraits of the Artist. Art J.* 49:182–86.

Dahl, H. (1965), Observations on a "natural experiment": Helen Keller. *J. Amer. Psychoanal. Assn.,* 13:533–50.

Detrick, D. & Detrick, S., ed. (1989), *Self Psychology.* Hillsdale, NJ: The Analytic Press.

Deutsch, F. (1949), *Applied Psychoanalysis.* New York: Grune & Stratton.

Dewald, P. (1981), Revision: yes. Improvement: no. *Psychoanal. Inq.,* 1:187–204.

Edelson, M. (1984), *Hypothesis and Evidence in Psychoanalysis.* Chicago: University of Chicago Press.

Eissler, K. (1953), The effect of the structure of the ego on psychoanalytic technique. *J. Amer. Psychoanal. Assn.,* 1:104–143.

_____ (1958), *Medical Orthodoxy and the Future of Psychoanalysis.* New York: International Universities Press.

Emde, R. (1983), The pre-representational self and its affective core. *The Psychoanalytic Study of the Child,* 38:165–192. New Haven, CT: Yale University Press.

Erikson, E. (1959), *Identity and the Life Cycle. Psychological Issues,* Monogr. 1. New York: International Universities Press.

Erle, J. (1979), An approach to the study of analyzability and analysis: The course of forty consecutive cases selected for supervised analyses. *Psychoanal. Quart.,* 48:198–228.

_____ & Goldberg, D. (1984), Observations on assessment of analyzability by experienced analysts. *J. Amer. Psychoanal. Assn.,* 32:715–38.

Fairbairn, W. (1954), *An Object Relations Theory of Personality.* New York: Basic Books.

Ferenczi, S. (1908–1933), *Bausteine zur Psychoanalyse.* Vols. 1 & 2. Leipzig/Wien/Zurich: Internationaler Psychoanalytischer Verlag, 1927; Vols. 3 & 4. Bern: Hans Huber, 1939.

_____ (1913), Stages in the development of the sense of reality. In: *Selected Papers of Sandor Ferenczi,* 3 volumes. New York: Basic Books, 1950–1955. Vol. 1, pp. 213–239.

_____ (1925), Contra-indications to the "active" psychoanalytical technique. In: *Selected Papers of Sandor Ferenczi,* 3 volumes. New York: Basic Books,

Vol. 2, pp. 217–230.

Firestein, S. (1978), *Termination in Psychoanalysis*. New York: International Universities Press.

Fraiberg, S. & Freedman, D. (1974), Studies in the ego development of the congenitally blind. *The Psychoanalytic Study of the Child*, 19:113–69. New York: International Universities Press.

Freedman, D. (1984), The origins of motivation. In: *Psychoanalysis: The Vital Issues*, Vol. 1, ed. J. Gedo & G. Pollock. New York: International Universities Press, pp. 17–38.

Freud, A. (1965), *Normality and Pathology in Childhood*. New York: International Universities Press.

_____ (1966), Obsessional neurosis: A summary of psychoanalytic views as presented at the [24th International] Congress [Amsterdam, July, 1965]. *Internat. J. Psychoanal.*, 47:116–22.

Freud, S. (1891), Sketches for the "preliminary communication" of 1893. *Standard Edition*, 1:147. London: Hogarth Press, 1966.

_____ (1895), Project for a scientific psychology. *Standard Edition*, 1:283–391. London: Hogarth Press, 1966.

_____ (1900), *The Interpretation of Dreams. Standard Edition*, 4 & 5. London: Hogarth Press, 1953.

_____ (1905a), Three essays on the theory of sexuality. *Standard Edition*, 7:130–243. London: Hogarth Press, 1953.

_____ (1905b), Fragment of an analysis of a case of hysteria. *Standard Edition*, 7:7–123. London: Hogarth Press, 1953.

_____ (1909a), Analysis of a phobia in a five-year-old boy. *Standard Edition*, 10:5–149. London: Hogarth Press, 1955.

_____ (1909b), Notes upon a case of obsessional neurosis. *Standard Edition*, 10:153–250. London: Hogarth Press, 1955.

_____ (1911–15), Papers on technique. *Standard Edition*, 12:85–171. London: Hogarth Press, 1958.

_____ (1913), Totem and taboo. *Standard Edition*, 13:1–162. London: Hogarth Press, 1955.

_____ (1914), On narcissism: An introduction. *Standard Edition*, 14:73–102. London: Hogarth Press, 1957.

_____ (1920), Beyond the pleasure principle. *Standard Edition*, 18:7–64. London: Hogarth Press, 1955.

_____ (1923), The ego and the id. *Standard Edition*, 19:12–59. London: Hogarth Press, 1961.

_____ (1926), Inhibitions, symptoms, and anxiety. *Standard Edition*, 20:87–172. London: Hogarth Press, 1959.

_____ (1937), Analysis terminable and interminable. *Standard Edition*, 23:216–53. London: Hogarth Press, 1964.

_____ (1977), Correspondence with Georg Groddeck. In: G. Groddeck, *The Meaning of Illness*. New York: International Universities Press.

Friedman, H. (1988), Review of John E. Gedo's *Conceptual Issues in Psychoanalysis*. *Internat. Rev. Psycho-Anal.*, 15:263–67.

Friedman, L. (1988), *The Anatomy of Psychotherapy*. Hillsdale, NJ: The Analytic Press.

Fromm-Reichmann, F. (1950), *Principles of Intensive Psychotherapy*. Chicago: University of Chicago Press.

Galatzer-Levy, R. (1986, May), Analytic experience with manic-depressive patients. Presented to the Chicago Psychoanalytic Society.

Gardner, R. (1983), *Self Inquiry*. Hillsdale, NJ: The Analytic Press, 1987.

———— (1987, Oct.), Some self-analytical reflections on self-analysis. Presented to the Chicago Psychoanalytic Society.

Gedo, J. (1964), Concepts for a classification of the psychotherapies. *Internat. J. Psycho-Anal.*, 45:530–39.

———— (1967), Noch einmal der gelehrte Säugling. *Psyche*, 22:301–309.

———— (1973), Kant's way: The psychoanalytic contribution of David Rapaport. *Psychoanal. Quart.*, 42:409–434.

———— (1975a), To Heinz Kohut: On his 60th birthday. *The Annual of Psychoanalysis*, 3:313–322. New York: International Universities Press.

———— (1975b), Forms of idealization in the analytic transference. *J. Amer. Psychoanal. Assn.*, 23:485–505.

———— (1977a), Notes on the psychoanalytic management of archaic transferences. *J. Amer. Psychoanal. Assn.*, 25:787–803.

———— (1977b), Review of George S. Klein's *Psychoanalytic Theory: An Exploration of Essentials* and Merton M. Gill & Philip S. Holzman's *Psychology Versus Metapsychology*, *Psychoanal. Quart.*, 46:319–25.

———— (1979a), *Beyond Interpretation*. New York: International Universities Press.

———— (1979b), A psychoanalyst reports at mid-career. *Amer. J. Psychiatry*, 136:646–649.

———— (1980), Reflections on some current controversies in psychoanalysis. *J. Amer. Psychoanal. Assn.*, 28:363–383.

———— (1981a), Measure for measure: A response. *Psychoanal. Inquiry*, 1:289–316.

———— (1981b), *Advances in Clinical Psychoanalysis*. New York: International Universities Press.

———— (1983), *Portraits of the Artist*. Hillsdale, NJ: The Analytic Press, 1989.

———— (1984), *Psychoanalysis and Its Discontents*. New York: Guilford.

———— (1986), *Conceptual Issues in Psychoanalysis*. Hillsdale, NJ: The Analytic Press.

———— (1988), *The Mind in Disorder*. Hillsdale, NJ: The Analytic Press.

———— (in press), Between reductionism and prolixity: Psychoanalysis and Occam's razor. *J. Amer. Psychoanal. Assn.*, 39.

———— & Goldberg, A. (1973), *Models of the Mind*. Chicago: University of Chicago Press.

Gedo, P. (1988), The significant hour in psychoanalysis: Insight and facilitative therapist interventions. Unpublished doctoral dissertation, Committee on Human Development, University of Chicago.

Gill, M. (1979), The analysis of the transference. *J. Amer. Psychoanal. Assn.*, 27 (Suppl.):263–88.

_____ (1981), The boundaries of psychoanalytic data and technique: A critique of Gedo's *Beyond Interpretation. Psychoanal. Inq.,* 1:205–232.

_____ (1983a), *The Analysis of the Transference,* Vol. 1. *Psychological Issues* Monogr. 53. New York: International Universities Press.

_____ (1983b), Review of John E. Gedo's *Advances in Clinical Psychoanalysis. Contemp. Psychol.,* 28:69–70.

_____ & Holzman, P., eds. (1976), *Psychology Versus Metapsychology, Psychological Issues* Monogr. 36. New York: International Universities Press.

Glover, E. (1931), The therapeutic effect of inexact interpretation: A contribution to the theory of suggestion. In: *The Technique of Psychoanalysis.* New York: International Universities Press, 1955, pp. 353–66.

Goldberg, A., ed. (1978), *The Psychology of the Self: A Casebook.* New York: International Universities Press.

Goldberg, D. (1984), Review of John E. Gedo's "Advances in Clinical Psychoanalysis." *Psychoanal. Quart.,* 53:83–89.

Gottesman, I. & Bertelsen, A. (1989), Confirming unexpressed genotypes in schizophrenia. *Arch. Gen. Psych.,* 46:867–72.

Grand, S., Freedman, N., Feiner, K. & Kiersky, S. (1988), Notes on the progressive and regressive shifts in levels of integrative failure. *Psychoanal. Contemp. Thought,* 11:705–740.

Grinker, R., McGregor, H., Selan, K., Klein, A. & Kohrman, J. (1961), *Psychiatric Social Work.* New York: Basic Books.

Grossman, W. (in press), Hierarchies, boundaries, and representation in a Freudian model of mental organization. *J. Amer. Psychoanal. Assn.*

Grünbaum, A. (1984), *The Foundations of Psychoanalysis.* Berkeley: University of California Press.

Gustafson, J. (1984), An integration of brief dynamic psychotherapy. *Amer. J. Psychiatry,* 141:935–944.

_____ (1986), *The Complex Secret of Brief Psychotherapy.* New York: Norton.

Hadley, J. (1985), Attention, affect, and attachment. *Psychoanal. Contemp. Thought,* 8:529–50.

_____ (1989), The neurobiology of motivational systems. In: *Psychoanalysis and Motivation,* by J. Lichtenberg, Hillsdale, NJ: The Analytic Press, pp. 337–372.

Hartmann, H. (1939), *Ego Psychology and the Problem of Adaptation.* New York: International Universities Press, 1958.

_____ (1964), *Essays in Ego Psychology.* New York: International Universities Press.

_____ Kris, E. & Loewenstein, R. (1964), *Papers on Psychoanalytic Psychology, Psychological Issues* Monogr. 14. New York: International Universities Press.

Harlow, H. (1962), The effect of rearing conditions on behavior. *Bull. Menninger Clin.,* 26:213–24.

Hook, S., ed. (1959), *Psychoanalysis, Scientific Method, and Philosophy.* New York: Grove Press.

Itard, J. (1802–06), *The Wild Boy of Aveyron,* trans. G. Humphrey & M. Humphrey. New York: Century, 1932.

Jackson, H. (1884), Evolution and dissolution of the nervous system. In: *Selected Writings of Hughlings Jackson,* J. Taylor, ed. New York: Basic Books, 1958.

Jaffe, D. (1984), Review of John E. Gedo's *Advances in Clinical Psychoanalysis. Internat. J. Psycho-Anal.,* 65:223–29.

Kantrowitz, J. (1987), Suitability for psychoanalysis. *Yearbook Psychoanal. Psychother.,* 2:403–15. New York: Guilford.

_____ Katz, A. & Paolitto, F. (1990), Follow-up of psychoanalysis five to ten years after termination: I. Stability of change. *J. Amer. Psychoanal. Assn.,* 38:471–96.

Kaplan, D. (1981), Review of John E. Gedo's *Beyond Interpretation. Psychoanal. Rev.,* 68:285–88.

Karasu, T. (1990), Toward a clinical model of psychotherapy for depression, I. Systematic comparison of three psychotherapies. *Amer. J. Psych.,* 147:133–47.

Khantzian, E. (1987, May), Substance dependence, repetition, and the nature of addictive suffering. Presented to the American Psychoanalytic Association.

Klein, G. (1976), *Psychoanalytic Theory.* New York: International Universities Press.

Klein, M. (1984), *Writings,* 4 volumes. New York: Free Press.

Kohut, H. (1959), Introspection, empathy, and psychoanalysis: An examination of the relationship between mode of observation and theory. In: *The Search for the Self.* Vol. 1, ed. P. Ornstein. New York: International Universities Press, 1978, pp. 205–232.

_____ (1966), Forms and transformations of narcissism. In: *The Search for the Self.* Vol. 1, ed. P. Ornstein. New York: International Universities Press, 1978, pp. 427–460.

_____ (1968), The psychoanalytic treatment of narcissistic personality disorders: Outline of a systematic approach. In: *The Search for the Self.* Vol. 1, ed. P. Ornstein. New York: International Universities Press, 1978, pp. 477–509.

_____ (1971), *The Analysis of the Self.* New York: International Universities Press.

_____ (1972), Thoughts on narcissism and narcissistic rage. In: *The Search for the Self.,* Vol. 2, ed. P. Ornstein. New York: International Universities Press, 1978, pp. 615–658.

_____ (1973), The future of psychoanalysis. In: *The Search for the Self,* Vol. 2, ed. P. Ornstein. New York: International Universities Press, 1978, pp. 663–84.

_____ (1976), Creativeness, charisma, group psychology. In: *The Search for the Self,* Vol. 2, ed. P. Ornstein. New York: International Universities Press, 1978, pp. 793–843.

_____ (1977), *The Restoration of the Self.* New York: International Universities Press.

_____ (1978), *The Search for the Self,* 2 vols., ed. P. Ornstein. New York: International Universities Press.

_____ (1980a), From a letter to one of the participants at the Chicago conference on the psychology of the self. In: *Advances in Self Psychology,* ed. A. Goldberg. New York: International Universities Press, pp. 449–456.

_____ (1980b), Reflections on *Advances in Self Psychology.* In: *Advances in Self Psychology,* ed. A. Goldberg. New York: International Universities Press, pp. 473–554.

_____ (1984), *How Does Analysis Cure?* ed. A. Goldberg & P. Stepansky. Chicago: University of Chicago Press.

_____ & Wolf, E. (1978), The disorders of the self and their treatment: An outline. *Internat. J. Psycho-Anal.,* 59:413–426.

Levin, F. (1991), *Mapping the Mind.* Hillsdale, NJ: The Analytic Press.

Lichtenberg, J. (1983), *Psychoanalysis and Infant Research.* Hillsdale, NJ: The Analytic Press.

_____ (1989), *Psychoanalysis and Motivation.* Hillsdale, NJ: The Analytic Press.

Lichtenstein, H. (1964), The role of narcissism in the emergence and maintenance of primary identity. *Internat. J. Psycho-Anal.,* 45:49–56.

_____ (1965), Towards a metapsychological definition of the concept of self. *Internat. J. Psycho-Anal.,* 46:117–128.

Loewald, H. (1989), *Sublimation.* New Haven, CT: Yale University Press.

Ludowyk-Gyömröi, E. (1963), The analysis of a young concentration camp victim. *The Psychoanalytic Study of the Child,* 18:484–510. New York: International Universities Press.

Malatesta, C. & Wilson, A. (1988), Emotion/cognition interaction in personality development: A discrete emotions, functionalist analysis. *Brit. J. Soc. Psychol.,* 27:91–112.

Mason, M. (1932), Learning to speak after 6-½ years of silence. *J. Speech & Hearing Disord.,* 7:295–304.

McLaughlin, J. (1983), Review of John E. Gedo's *Beyond Interpretation. Psychoanal. Quart.,* 52:271–80.

Modell, A. (1965), On having the right to a life: An aspect of the superego's development. *Internat. J. Psycho-Anal.,* 46:323–31.

_____ (1968), *Object Love and Reality.* New York: International Universities Press.

_____ (1974), Review of John E. Gedo & Arnold Goldberg's *Models of the Mind. Psychoanal. Quart.,* 43:674–77.

_____ (1976), "The holding environment" and the therapeutic action of psychoanalysis. *J. Amer. Psychoanal. Assn.,* 24:285–308.

_____ (1983, Oct.), The two contexts of the self. Presented to the 50th Anniversary Symposium, Boston Psychoanalytic Society and Institute.

_____ (1984), *Psychoanalysis in a New Context.* New York: International Universities Press.

Moraitis, G. (in press). Phobias and the pursuit of novelty. *Psychoanal. Inq.,* 11:296–315..

Opatow, B. (1989), Drive theory and the metapsychology of experience. *Internat. J. Psych-Anal.,* 70:645–60.

Panel (1971), Models of the psychic apparatus, S. Abrams, reporter. *J. Amer. Psychoanal. Assn.,* 19:132–142.

Panel (1976), New horizons in metapsychology, W. Meissner, reporter. *J. Amer. Psychoanal. Assn.,* 24:161–180.

Panel (in prep.), Obsessional phenomena, J. Robinson, reporter.

Piaget, J. (1971), *Biology and Knowledge.* Chicago: University of Chicago Press.

Pine, F. (1989), *Drive, Ego, Object, Self.* New York: Basic Books.

Polányi, M. (1974), *Scientific Thought and Social Reality.* New York: International Universities Press.

Rangell, L. (1981), A view on John Gedo's revision of psychoanalytic theory. *Psychoanal. Inq.,* 1:249–66.

Rapaport, D. (1951), *The Organization and Pathology of Thought.* New York: Columbia University Press.

_____ (1960), *The Structure of Psychoanalytic Theory. Psychological Issues* Monogr. 6. New York: International Universities Press.

_____ (1967), *The Collected Papers of David Rapaport,* ed. M. Gill. New York: Basic Books.

_____ (1974), *The History of the Concept of Association of Ideas.* New York: International Universities Press.

Rappaport, E. (1960), Preparation for analysis. *Internat. J. Psycho-Anal.,* 41:626–32.

Reed, G. (1985), Review of John E. Gedo's *Psychoanalysis and Its Discontents. Psychoanal. Assn. of N.Y. Bull.,* 23:3/4, 10–11.

Richards, A. (1981), Review of John E. Gedo's *Beyond Interpretation. Psychoanal. Assn. of N.Y. Bull.,* 18:2, 5–7.

Rieff, P. (1966), *The Triumph of the Therapeutic.* New York: Viking Press.

Robbins, M. (1983), Toward a new mind model for the primitive personalities. *Internat. J. Psycho-Anal.,* 64:127–148.

_____ (1987, May), Broadening the scope of psychoanalysis to include more seriously disturbed individuals. Presented to the American Academy of Psychoanalysis, Chicago.

_____ (1988, Oct.), Discussion of John Gedo's *The Mind in Disorder.* Presented to the Boston Psychoanalytic Society.

Rodgers, T. (1990), Review of John E. Gedo's *The Mind in Disorder. Psychoanal. Books,* 1:192–203.

Rosenblatt, A. & Thickstun, J. (1977), *Modern Psychoanalytic Concepts in a General Psychology. Psychological Issues,* Monogr. 42/43. New York: International Universities Press.

Rubinstein, B. (1974), On the role of classificatory processes in mental functioning: Aspects of a psychoanalytic theoretical model. *Psychoanal. & Contemp. Science,* 3:101–185.

_____ (1976), On the possibility of a strictly clinical psychoanalytic theory: An essay in the philosophy of psychoanalysis. *Psychology versus Metapsychology, Psychological Issues* Monogr. 36, ed. M. Gill & P. Holzman. New York: International Universities Press, pp. 229–264.

Schafer, R. (1976), *A New Language for Psychoanalysis.* New Haven, CT: Yale University Press.

Schwaber, E. (1987), Review of *Kohut's Legacy. J. Amer. Psychoanal. Assn.,* 35:743–750.

Schwartz, A. (1987), Drives, affects, behavior and learning: Approaches to a psychobiology of emotion and to an integration of psychoanalytic and neurobiologic thought. *J. Amer. Psychoanal. Assn.*, 35:467–506.

Searles, H. (1986), *My Work with Borderline Patients*. Northvale, NJ: Aronson.

Segal, H. & Britton, R. (1981), Interpretation and primitive psychic processes: A Kleinian view. *Psychoanal. Inq.*, 1:267–78.

Silverman, D. & Silverman, L. (1983), Review of John E. Gedo's *Advances in Clinical Psychoanalysis. Rev. Psychoanal. Books*, 2:321–40.

Stepansky, P. (1983), *In Freud's Shadow*. Hillsdale, NJ: The Analytic Press.

Stern, D. (1985), *The Interpersonal World of the Infant*. New York: Basic Books.

_____ (1987, April), The dialectic between the "interpersonal" and the "intrapsychic": With particular emphasis on the role of memory and representation. Presented at the 50th Anniversary Symposium of the Washington School of Psychiatry.

Stone, L. (1965), *The Psychoanalytic Situation*. New York: International Universities Press.

Sullivan, H. (1940), *Conceptions of Modern Psychiatry*. Washington, DC: W.A. White Psychiatric Foundation.

_____ (1956), *Clinical Studies in Psychiatry*. New York: Norton.

Sulloway, F. (1979), *Freud, Biologist of the Mind*. New York: Basic Books.

Tarachow, S. (1963), *An Introduction to Psychotherapy*. New York: International Universities Press.

Terman, D. (1976, December), Distortions of the Oedipus complex in severe pathology: Some vicissitudes of self development and their relationship to the Oedipus complex. Presented to the American Psychoanalytic Association, New York.

_____ (1984/85), The self and the Oedipus complex. *The Annual of Psychoanalysis*, 12/13:87–104. New York: International Universities Press.

Turkle, S. (1978), *Psychoanalytic Politics*. New York: Basic Books.

Wallerstein, R. (1986a), *42 Lives in Treatment*. New York: Guilford.

_____ (1986b), Review of John E. Gedo's *Psychoanalysis and Its Discontents. Psychoanal. Quart.*, 63:323–34.

Winnicott, D. (1951), Transitional objects and transitional phenomena. In: *Collected Papers*. London: Tavistock, 1958, pp. 229–242.

_____ (1952), Psychoses and child care. In: *Collected Papers*. London: Tavistock, 1958, pp. 219–228.

_____ (1954), Metapsychological and clinical aspects of regression in the psycho-analytical set-up. In: *Collected Papers*. London: Tavistock, 1958, pp. 278–294.

_____ (1958), *Collected Papers*. London: Tavistock.

_____ (1965), *The Maturational Processes and the Facilitating Environment*. New York: International Universities Press.

Wolf, E. (1976), Ambience and abstinence. *The Annual of Psychoanalysis*. 4:101–115. New York: International Universities Press.

Zetzel, E. (1968), The so-called good hysteric. *Internat. J. Psycho-Anal.*, 49:256–260.

Name Index

Subject Index